Advance Praise

"Both during my career in law enforcement and after 30 years spent presenting the Good Knight Crime and Violence Prevention program in public school systems around the country I have seen far too many children struggling because they didn't fit into society's norms. I applaud Mara's new book, *Help! My Child Hates School*, for its groundbreaking exploration into the psychology of these misunderstood and gifted children.

"I hated school growing up because of being different. I was often bullied and criticized by teachers who said, 'Eddie you won't grow up to be anything.' I always answered, 'No I will grow up to be like a farmer out-standing in his field.' They didn't get it, but I did grow up to be knighted by a governor and received a distinguished award in the Oval Office!

"Mara's book is a must have family resource for all parents who care about our children. Remember understanding is the first step toward finding solutions."

-Sir Edward-Michael Jagen PhD, acclaimed author, child protection activist and founder of the Good Knight Child Empowerment Network Inc., a 501c3 non-profit.

"This book is an INVALUABLE resource for figuring out how to get your thriving child in an antiquated school system, or to do whatever's necessary to find your child's unique work around. I can't recommend this book any more highly. Written with heart and knowledge, this book will surely make your life better, and perhaps more importantly, get your child the experience they deserve - one where they are valued and stimulated to a lifelong love of learning, rather than simply existing as a round peg getting pounded into a square hole!

-Sandi Phillips Meyler, Coach, and author of *On the Road with Abraham: Master Manifestation and Create a Kick-Ass Life*

"Writing with passion and compassion, and conversing directly with the parent-reader throughout, the author of this book – an experienced and committed educator with a lifelong love of learning and an insider knowledge of the "big system of school" – sets out to empower parents of children who 'hate school' to identify what is really going on and to craft a solution.

"From the outset she makes clear that she will be the guide at the side at every step of this new parent-child 'learning adventure' that will take the child to a 'magic' place of lifelong love of learning. She does this by walking the parent through some simple diagnostic activities to complete with the child, reviewing all the learning options currently available, devising an action plan for change, and providing information and guidance and real life examples to help refine the choice of the best fit for the child.

"A concise summary and clear signposting at the start of each chapter help keep the adventurers on track, while the inclusion of an appendix listing the most common fears and FAQs parents have while making an educational change on behalf of their child lends added force to the book's plea to advocate for the child as a unique learner.

"This book is 'really all about fit,' a fit between the learning space and the child's innate love of learning. It will give all parents food for thought."

-Marie Martin Ed.D., Education Consultant, and author of *Learning by Wandering: An Ancient Irish Perspective for a Digital World*

"*HELP! My Child Hates School* is a wonderful guide for parents in that frustrating and scary situation. Mara's connection with children and experience with schools and families in this boat make her an excellent source of reliable information and the actual HELP to get your child happy, thriving, and loving learning again."

-Esther Goldenberg, Coach and Author of
*Resistant to Reading: Tricks and Tips for Parents
of Reluctant Readers*

"As a 29-year veteran holistic health and wellness practitioner I have seen firsthand the ravages of childhood trauma carried into adult life. Most of which is based on miscommunication between children and their parents. Even more importantly as a mother of three, with a 24-year span between the second and third child, I have a broad perspective on what we should place importance upon, in the raising of a child.

"Mara's book is an invaluable resource that allows for compassionate understanding to enter into the decision making process adults can use to fully guide their child's education. Awakening to the subtle wisdoms being shared in a child's words and actions, can help parents to avoid the tears and subsequent trauma experienced by children facing disconnected and seemingly endless classwork and homework."

-Sophia Key West, Holistic Wellness Practitioner, Reiki
Master, Crania-Sacral therapist, Certified Aromatherapist,
and author of *When Angels Dream: Book of the North
(Diary of an Angel Knight, Volume 1)*

HELP! My Child Hates School

HELP!
My Child Hates School

An Awakened Parent's
Guide to Action

MARA LINABERGER, ED.D.

NEW YORK

NASHVILLE • MELBOURNE • VANCOUVER

HELP! My Child Hates School

An Awakened Parent's Guide to Action

Published in New York, New York, by Morgan James Publishing in partnership with Difference Press. Morgan James is a trademark of Morgan James, LLC. www.MorganJamesPublishing.com

The Morgan James Speakers Group can bring authors to your live event. For more information or to book an event visit The Morgan James Speakers Group at www.TheMorganJamesSpeakersGroup.com.

ISBN 9781683506393 paperback
ISBN 9781683506409 eBook
Library of Congress Control Number: 2017909704

Cover Design by:
Jennifer Stimson

Interior Design by:
Chris Treccani
www.3dogcreative.net

In an effort to support local communities, raise awareness and funds, Morgan James Publishing donates a percentage of all book sales for the life of each book to Habitat for Humanity Peninsula and Greater Williamsburg.

Get involved today! Visit
www.MorganJamesBuilds.com

For Monica and Angela

wisdom teachers of the highest order

incredible bookends to my first book

Table of Contents

Foreword

Where were thinkers like Mara Linaberger when I was a child? Who spoke up then for those who were different, odd, or just didn't fit in?

I come from an era where dyslexia and synesthesia (sensing in multiples) were unknown, the horror of Pearl Harbor an adults-only affair, and children – well – they existed solely as innocent bundles of curiosity ready to be molded into whatever society expected. Exceptions did not exist. Being the only child in the first grade who could see music, hear numbers, and smell color meant I was a liar. My punishment: sitting atop a tall stool in front of the class and on occasion wearing a conical hat that said "Dunce" on it as an example of a bad child who told lies. This turned my world upside down: for whenever I told the truth I was punished and whenever I lied I was praised. I eventually fled into nature for solace.

Each day when walking to school I passed home after home with gold stars in front room windows. Pearl Harbor! Those gold stars meant someone in that home had died in the war effort. Overnight a particular place had six new gold stars. Kids know what's going on. I stood there and sobbed and sobbed. I do not recall a single morning in all of first grade when I did not have to quiet my sobs and control my shudders just to walk in the door of my classroom. Throughout my school years I never understood why teachers gave kids a gold star for a correct paper. Gold meant death to me, so I did everything I could to ensure I never got 100% on assignments. It took until I was 50 years old before I could tolerate gold; my sixties before I could wear the stuff.

The nightmare of my first grade determined not only the way I would live my life, but how I raised my children: never to trust authorities – always find your own truth yourself. You might say I became a crusader.

My story directly relates to this book. Back in the forties, parents had no choice where to send their kids to school, and teachers had virtually no choice in how to teach. Only a very different type of classroom format would have enabled me to learn without fear and retribution. Only in a school where philosophy was taught (this could and should be offered in elementary school, read Little Big Minds by Marietta McCarty) could I have dealt with war, my neighbors dying, air raid drills, rationing, and the Saturday morning movies that billed Hitler on the same stage as Roy Rogers. Good and evil? How can kids deal with this? In today's news, you find the same conundrum.

This book in a most unique way gives you tools, as it shows you as a parent that you have a choice of where and how you educate your children. Kids are different now, at least most of them. Some are born "knowing" more than their parents, and possess a capacity to learn that is almost unheard of. The cyber world quite literally is altering brain structure and brain function, leaving behind what makes us human. Those who can't keep up, ideologies that clash… spill out across living rooms everywhere there is television or access to the Internet. Kids see this, and they shudder just like I did when bombs fell at Pearl Harbor. Children must talk. And they must be heard: their fears and questions addressed.

This is a book about choices. Yes, about what's "out there," but equally important about how to determine what type of learner you have. Know your child! Parents think they do. Most do not. Until you spend time with your son or daughter, talking, exploring, listening, you really don't know what he or she wants or what might work best in this new world of education.

You'll gain options, plus ways to narrow your search – even considering family income. If you think children today do not face the horrors I once did, take a look at what's happening in Chicago, Philadelphia, Austin, Los Angeles. Just walking to school can still be a test of faith.

Choice! This book is dedicated to helping parents enable their children to flourish as the unique wonder they are. What a different life I could have had, had anyone bothered to "see me," be they parent ... or educator.

P. M. H. Atwater, L.H.D.,
Researcher of Near-Death States and Evolutionary Cycles.
Author of such books as: ***Children of the Fifth World, Future Memory, Dying to Know You: Proof of God in the Near-Death Experience***, and ***A Manual for Developing Humans***.

Introduction

> *"We ask children to do for most of a day what few adults are*
> *able to do even for an hour. How many of us, attending, say,*
> *a lecture that doesn't interest us, can keep our minds from*
> *wandering?"*
> - **John Holt**, How Children Learn ... and Fail

Have you ever searched the Internet for any of the following questions or phrases?

- Help! My kid hates school!
- How can I make my kid go to (or like) school?
- Why do I have to send my kid to school anyway?
- What happens if my kid doesn't go to school?
- What's wrong with school?

If so, I believe we've been brought together for a very specific purpose at this precise moment in time. As a professional educator turned educational consultant, I've spent a *lot* of time thinking about why school doesn't work for everyone. One of my main goals in writing this book is to help you tackle those questions too, in a positive, life-affirming, and life-changing way. I'm thrilled you've chosen to join me on this grand adventure!

My kid hates school.

If you've actually done a search on this phrase, you may already realize your child's statement is not what it appears to be on the surface. Kids use the word "hate" all the time to draw attention to things that don't feel right or to things that aren't working. Hate is classically defined as *having a strong or intense dislike of something.*

Your child's use of the word hate is actually an attempt to get your attention, to let you know that something is out of alignment at school. More often than not, hatred of school comes from complete frustration with how things feel to your child. Getting to the bottom of these feelings is key to coming up with a cure, to crafting a solution for your child that helps recapture his natural-born curiosity and love of learning.

Can you remember when your child was a baby? How curious she was, putting things in her mouth to taste them as she began to investigate the world at her fingertips? Remember how he scooted, crawled, and then took his first steps by pulling himself up and letting go in order to walk? In those formative moments of your child's young life, your son was curious, inquisitive, and passionate about learning. The world was his classroom. Your daughter didn't come to you for answers so much as she watched you closely to see what she could learn for herself. When it came to talking, you didn't teach her to speak through formal lessons, but rather by encouraging her first attempts to speak.

Think about it: school, in general, looks very little like this wild, free, individual, and collaborative exploration of life that is the hallmark of being a baby and toddler. What if learning could be more like that childlike wonder we all once had?

What triggers your child? What makes her hate school? Let's take a look at some of the most common sources. They include complaints such as:

- early school start times
- too much time spent sitting at an individual desk
- too much content "squeezed in" too fast, or concepts that are difficult to grasp
- content that is too easy, presented too slowly, or in a boring way
- lengthy or confusing homework that feels like "busywork"
- an increased focus on test prep and testing vs. learning
- elimination of recess, art, music, and/or PE
- being bullied, feeling different, invisible, or like an outcast
- overcrowding, too many kids, too many needs for individualization to occur
- fear, or an activation of the "fight or flight" response

Digging deeper behind those initial concerns, there are legitimate reasons behind your child's complaints. Some of the deeper sources of pain for your child may include:

- your child's biological clock operates differently than the school's hours of operation
- your child may crave more physical and kinesthetic movement in order to learn
- there may be little time spent on creativity, imagination, and invention
- learning of content may not fit your child's need, interest, or preference for pace
- your child may need to decompress, relax, and rejuvenate at the end of the day

- your child may have a sense that tests and grades are what are valued by adults
- your child may feel punished when his favorite creative outlets are being reduced
- your child may feel that he doesn't belong, isn't seen or heard, and doesn't fit in
- your child may feel more like a number than an individual
- and in the worst case, your child may no longer feel safe, cared for, or welcome at school

Do any of the items on these two lists ring true for your child? So often a child's dislike of school boils down to the simple fact that something is not a good fit to who he or she is as a unique individual. Sit with that a moment. It's really all about fit. When you have a pair of shoes that rub a blister or feel too tight, you put on another pair, loosen the laces, or just plain take them off, don't you? You don't blame your feet for the pain, and you don't try to make your feet fit in. You look at the source of the pain and make a change for the better. You search for a pair of shoes that *do* fit.

While finding the right fit for your child may take some time and effort on your part, doesn't it feel good to know that the underlying problem is a singular one? That your child's school somehow doesn't fit and that you can quickly figure out *what would work better* for your child?

Throughout this book, we are going tackle this source of pain for your child, much like a detective might when solving a complex mystery. We will walk through some simple activities to complete with your child to figure out what is really going on. Then we'll review all of the learning options available today. The field of possibilities is pretty complex, but we'll check out the broad categories to get you honed in on options that are the best fit for your child. Finally we will create a plan of action for you to put into motion. Examining school and learning choices is much like that shoe metaphor. You may choose to loosen the shoes you've got on, try on a brand new pair, or skip wearing shoes all together. There isn't one right solution for anything. There isn't a single type of school that works for everyone, so we'll cover all the bases to make sure you have the data you need to make an informed decision for your child. Another overarching goal of this book is to help you begin to understand how the big system of school works, and what you can do to create change. You'll learn some tips and tricks to help you play the game of school your way. The choices and action steps you take will stem from a deep knowing of and collaboration with your child. The road may be bumpy at times. But hey, what's that old Einstein quote about the definition of insanity? Doing the same things over and over again, but expecting a different result? One thing's for sure, if you are reading this book, you are ready to try something different. And you are most assuredly not insane.

How can I make my kid go to (or like) school?

This is a bit of a loaded question. My usual response when parents ask it is: does it make sense to try and get your child to like something that he hates? How does it make you feel to have to do things that you hate? Yes, this book will include lots of strategies to clarify your child's likes and dislikes related to school and learning. You may choose to use that knowledge in order to more effectively advocate for your child at school. That single action can make a significant difference in your child's emotional state and experience. We'll also touch on some techniques your child can use to identify the stressors and cultivate a more peaceful mind-state at school as well as at home. You may find as you work through the activities with your child, that his or her current school isn't the best fit. So we'll examine the wide variety of educational options available to help you make a choice that will help rebuild your child's love of learning.

Why do I have to send my kid to school anyway?

There are some valid reasons for your child to go to school. Learning the basic skills needed to function as an informed citizen of the country includes learning to read, write, and communicate effectively, as well as being able to do simple math. The founding fathers of the United States intended school to be a great unifier for our country and its diverse immigrants, ensuring that everyone had an equal opportunity to be a part of the democratic process. Historically, many parents feel unqualified to teach those foundational basics, and so school has become a generally unquestioned rite of passage most require their children to participate in. Twelve years of school was the pattern many of our parents experienced, and most of us send our kids to school without question. In the US, legally, your child must take part in some sort form of approved education, which no longer requires attendance at a formal school.

What happens if my kid doesn't go to school?

While federal and state laws guide education, it is local government that is charged with the implementation of education. If your child doesn't attend the legally required number of days each year, you'll likely face truancy processes. These can vary from state to state, but generally include a progressive series of consequences. They often begin with a phone call, and move on to fines, a visit to the magistrate, required parenting classes, or even the threat of incarceration for you or your child when things are farther along. If you're unsure about the regulations in your area, you can ask your school's principal for the specifics on attendance and truancy, or you can locate the information on your district's website.

The legal measures truancy officers use to force your child to return to school are not a pleasant experience. If you're reading this book, it's possible that you or your child, on some level, see school as a prison. Isn't it strange that the solution to truancy is to threaten you and your child with fines and possible imprisonment? Sounds very much like a no-win situation.

You do have options. There are ways to make school more bearable, or even enjoyable. When school just isn't working for your child anymore, there is actually a ray of hope. You are capable of making a change that will feel much better to your child!

What's wrong with school?

Beyond the basics, our current system of education has added on a vast array of required content ("curriculum" in education-speak) to be mastered by your child. Many of the subjects that are required of today's student go far beyond what you and I were offered in school. And they are even more complex than the subjects studied in the day of the one-room schoolhouse. School has become a system that actually prolongs a young person's entry into the work world. With the US Department of Education's directive for every child to be college ready, a young person's educational preparation could now span 17 years (13 years of primary and secondary education, added to the four years typically needed to complete college)!

Certainly, school has served the purpose of increasing the opportunities for millions of students to learn and grow. And for most the costs have remained personally low, being sourced from the collection of real estate taxes. But for many families, school has become little more than a glorified childcare service. Many parents do not question the purpose behind compulsory education, nor do they stop to consider the implications of sending their child to school for 7-8 hours per day, 180 days a year, for 13 years. Because of the economic pressures on parents to work hard to earn the means to fulfill their own version of American Dream, many are unable to consider alternative options. Where parents once had the option to send their kids to school, most now assume they must. Or worse, they do it because they feel they have no other choice. This is not the whole truth. Rather, it's a mindset that can actually be changed.

Each day you dutifully send your child off to school where the staff legally functions on behalf of your child "in loco parentis," which means "in the place of the parent." If you watch the news, you've seen sad stories repeated over and over. Kids are being taught by teachers who are overwhelmed, stressed out, overworked, underpaid, or, even worse, incompetent. Yes, there are many excellent teachers out there. Sadly, many teachers do not stay in the profession beyond the first five years. And for those who do stay, most report greater stress and difficulty managing the increasing challenges of the classroom. While most teachers go into teaching because of a calling to be of service to children, many (myself included) become burned out by the demands of high-stakes testing, national standards, expanded curriculum, and evaluation pressures. One big factor in your child's dislike of school could well be the high stress levels of his or her teacher.

Statistics on student bullying, violence, and dropout rates don't paint a pretty picture of education either. From Columbine to Newtown, our children's school experiences are very different from those we remember. To enter a school today, adults must present an ID, sign in, and often pass through a metal detector. The days of your walking unannounced into school to bring cupcakes for a party are long gone, as are the blissful opportunities to attend a whole school performance in the auditorium. And opportunities to leave the school on field trips are almost nonexistent, unless teachers provide adequate documentation to administration supporting direct ties to curriculum standards.

All children, while equal in their right to a free public education, were not created equal in their likes, dislikes, passions, and sense of purpose in the world. Not all children learn to read at the same time, or even like to read. Not all kids are strong in math and science. Not all kids like to sit at a desk. What is common to all kids is an authentic uniqueness, a particular set of special gifts, and inherent genius, which often goes untapped in school. This book will help you identify and tap into your child's own special passion and genius, supporting him in finding the best educational setting possible for his growth and development. It will ask you to keep going, keep searching, and keep trying out settings until you find the place where your kid is finally happy, healthy, and flourishing!

If you still need further evidence that school isn't the haven it used to be, look no further than the wildly popular TED Talk by Sir Ken Robinson entitled: *How Schools Kill Creativity*. We live in a world that is changing rapidly, and we must begin to advocate for each child's freedom to learn in new, creative, and cooperative ways.

Why choose me as your guide?

What makes me qualified to serve as your guide on this wild adventure? What authority do I possess to ask you to stand up for your child in a system designed to keep you quiet and to teach your child to conform? Like your child, I struggled in my own love-hate relationship with school. In writing this book, I'm combining my prior school experiences with newly honed skills in a "make it up as you go along" lifestyle, to help you move forward in new and exciting ways.

Approximately four years ago, I lost my job after nearly 25 years in the big system of education. Like so many, I was downsized during a budget crisis. It was an extremely painful experience, psychologically, emotionally, and financially. But it was also a real moment of awakening for me, and it is a key reason I've chosen to write this book right now. In the fallout of my job loss, I began to ask questions about why school is the way it is and what it was designed to do. I investigated the history of education and found some startling information. It was hard to deal with the knowledge that I had become part of the system, part of the problem. Then I came to the conclusion that I could better tackle the big issues in education by working outside of the system, so I created my own business.

At night I began dreaming about teaching in a one-room schoolhouse. At first I was sure this was just a fantasy, my mind playing tricks on me, and that such schools no longer existed. To my great surprise, I found out that there are actually a few one-room schools still functioning. And I actually taught briefly in one on an island off the coast of Maine. The main thing I want to share about the past four years is that I've learned to follow my heart, and to look for the breadcrumbs along the way that point toward a more joyful and free kind of learning experience for today's kids. My plan is to teach you how to do that too.

One of my strongest and best skills is the ability see and know kids deeply. When I walked into a coffee shop the other day, a little girl of about two turned and looked right at me. I smiled back at her and she pointed to something outside. I laughed and said hello to her mom, sharing that I'd been a teacher for many years and that kids often talk with me because they know I can see them, and that I'm "safe."

A dear friend said to me the other day, "Mara, you know you are like a child whisperer. I've watched you do it." What I think she was pointing to was my ability to be fully present with a kid to see the things that makes him light up, to hear the joy in his voice, and to understand and draw out the excitement and passion as pointers on an authentic life path. She's been there and watched as I listen to parents and kids, guiding them to find the best educational setting possible for the child. This book is my way of cultivating those skill sets in you. You'll get to know more about your child as a learner and help her fall back in love with learning again. Together we'll rebuild her curiosity about the world that rivals her early childhood years and make sure that she knows she has access to learning wherever she goes!

We're going to cover a lot of ground together in the pages to follow. It's my recommendation that you consider keeping a notebook of your thoughts and ideas as you read forward. Let's begin!

Chapter 1

Where's the Magic?

"And above all, watch with glittering eyes the whole world around you because the greatest secrets are always hidden in the most unlikely places. Those who don't believe in magic will never find it."
-Roald Dahl, *The Minpins*

A s I began writing this book, I thought back to my days in school to see if there was some connection between my passion for educational alternatives and the trajectory of my career path. I've learned lots about myself and *following the magic,* choosing to do what feels good versus what is expected. I found that I've actually been preparing to write this book for a very long time. I wondered if there was some additional deep reason I feel called to help parents navigate school

1

issues with their children at this particular point in my life. Indeed there is a pattern.

My story is pretty typical, as far as an idyllic childhood in the 70s and 80s is concerned. I was born to two parents who had both attended college. I lived with them, my two sisters, and my maternal grandmother in her house. It was a traditional, colonial brick home on one acre of land where we had gardens, fruit trees, and lots of freedom. We also had extended family living next door and the other set of grandparents living close by.

I was a decent student, earning mostly As and Bs with the occasional C, usually in math or social studies. I played Suzuki violin, sang in the church choir from second grade onward, rode bikes, played in the sandbox or on the tire swing, and chose Legos or Play-Doh when I had to be inside. Recently I dug out the report cards my mother had saved for me, wondering if they'd shed any light upon my experiences at school. In the margins I noticed a lot of absences, and scattered comments about my need for improvement in the areas of taking constructive criticism and following directions. This was my first reminder of my own challenges with school.

I was fascinated to note that the other mementos of childhood school years my mother kept for me had less to do with school and more to do with extracurricular activities. There were programs from various church productions and from Suzuki violin recitals. And there were handmade playbills from the original dramatic productions my sisters and I put on for family on the Fourth of July with our cousins from Chicago.

This trip back in time clarified for me that when it came to school, I didn't always apply myself deeply in mastering the content teachers presented. I was often bored, engaging in my own fun by chatting with the other students nearby. As a handwritten comment on my report card pointed out in fifth grade, "Your work is good, but it could be so much better if you focused. Pay attention!" At the time I found these remarks confusing. Having been seated in groups, I found it difficult to limit my conversations with classmates to only those times deemed appropriate by the teacher.

Does this sound familiar? Are there any similarities to the comments made about you as a child or to your child?

As a kid I knew that I wanted to do what I wanted to do, when I wanted to do it. I'm pretty much the same gal today. Back then, when I voiced my desires with that simple clarity, most adults responded with something like, "Don't be silly, that's selfish." Others said, "You're too strong-willed, you need to learn to fit in." And I listened. Sigh. I tried my best to conform, but it was hard and I often fought back unconsciously. I ended up having lots of anxiety about complying with what I was being asked to do while trying to remain true to myself. At some point I gave up, as so many of us do, and conformed as often as I could to get through childhood and adolescence. It wasn't until college that I began to reawaken, exploring my own inner urgings, creating a path I loved.

When you think back, what do you remember about school? Is there a pattern to your memories? I recall very little of the specifics around school days, and almost nothing about what I was directly taught. Most of my memories revolve around things that felt good, magical. For instance, I remember my third-grade teacher who read *The Last of the Really Great Whangdoodles* after lunch every day, and the fifth-grade teacher who helped us put on two plays: "Mr. Grumpy's Toyshop" and "The Saga of Dead Dog Gulch." I recall the middle-school science teacher who bought a pigeon and a fetal pig when a classmate and I asked to do more investigations in animal dissection. (Ick, what was I thinking!) What my memories have in common is that they center around teachers who fed my imagination and who created space and validity for me to explore the things that I loved the most.

Whether we realize it or not, *what we value the most, we make time for.* The teachers I remember with fondness are those who made time for the things that I loved. They are the ones that encouraged my curiosity. They validated the importance of literature, arts, and hands-on exploration, and the things that brought learning to life. What kinds of learning do you value most? How about your child?

When I hit college, it was the small class sizes and the freedom to choose my own coursework that really jazzed me up. I tried on English, then Information Science, and finally settled on Psychology as my major. I found my way in to education as a career by completing a master of arts in teaching the year after graduation. I'd been babysitting for my advisor and she suggested the career path based on my deep connection to and natural talent with her own children.

Amazingly, fun followed me into the arena of work, though I couldn't always see it at the very beginning. Three long years as a day-to-day substitute teacher in the inner city schools nearly crushed my desire to teach. But eventually a long-term sub position led to my first contract as a kindergarten teacher. I began teaching in two buildings, finally landing permanently in a single building after commuting at noon every day. Amazingly, my first full-time classroom position was in the same building and classroom in which my maternal grandmother had taught music in forty years earlier. How's that for following the magic!

The building I taught in for over 17 years started out as a traditional academy magnet, a school choice alternative for families that focused on classical academics and required kids to wear uniforms. Because of a lottery system and requirements for racial balance, my classes were rich and diverse. A few years in, we morphed into an arts and humanities magnet, infusing our school with rich visual arts, music, dance, and theater opportunities. It was a glorious place to be. Most days it didn't feel like work at all, it was more like being paid to explore and learn alongside children all day.

What made working at this school extra special was the convergence of several key elements. We were led by a principal who was able to see the unique talents that each of us possessed and play to them. Bob was a master at helping each teacher find his or her gifts and at nurturing each teacher's personal creativity. Under his tutelage, I had a chance to teach first grade and third grade, open a writing center, and run the new computer lab as a technology mentor. And he provided us with rich opportunities to expand our own learning in creative writing, advanced questioning techniques, and arts integration. What made Bob so special was that he saw us as individuals, not as mere cogs in the wheel or slaves to the system. It was an amazing opportunity to serve and learn with him.

Even with all the opportunities this special principal provided, I can still remember having my doubts about the direction education was heading. First came the seemingly impossible goals of the legislation known as "No Child Left Behind," which demanded 100% proficiency from all students within a ten-year timeframe. Then came my seriously considering quitting. I had several students fail to learn to read, which required their retention in first grade. I felt like a failure. It was a caring colleague who urged me to look at how many kids had succeeded, and also to consider trying teaching at another grade level.

Sometimes I kept myself going by imagining working my way up in the system and making a difference as a leader. It was another colleague who suggested that I might make a great principal. When I looked at the work my principal was doing up close, it didn't look like much fun to me! While I decided I wasn't interested in leading a school, my colleague's suggestion actually inspired me to do graduate work in instructional technology. Going back to grad school added to my skillset as a teacher, ultimately allowing me to morph myself into the trainer, mentor, and coach that I am today.

What I learned along the pathway of school to a career in education are guideposts and skills that I can share with you as a parent. Sure, I know lots about curriculum, standards, and assessments. I also know *that they aren't the most important part of learning.* I've learned that honoring a student where and as they are in the moment is the first step to helping them develop a love of learning. As I said before, what we focus on is what is most important to us, so putting your child first is what's most important when it comes to education.

In coming chapters, I'll share ways to get to know your child deeply as a unique learner. You'll learn how to help them recognize their own passions as a guide to direct their steps forward in life. I've personally learned how to identify and follow the magic and how to see endings as opportunities for new beginnings. And, perhaps most importantly, I've learned how to chart my own path as a life-long learner. Nowadays, I spend most of my time deeply engaged with content related to my clients and my own personal growth. I've written this book to assist you in helping your child develop this sort of life-long love affair with learning.

Chapter 2

What's Wrong with School?

"Children learn what they live. Put kids in a class and they will
live out their lives in an invisible cage, isolated from their chance
at community; interrupt kids with bells and horns all the time
and they will learn that nothing is important or worth finishing;
ridicule them and they will retreat from human association;
shame them and they will find a hundred ways to get even. The
habits taught in large- scale organizations are deadly."
-John Taylor Gatto, *The Underground History of Education*

D id Gatto's words speak to you as they did to me the first time
I read them? In what way? Does your child ever come home
from school reporting that it feels isolating or prison-like, that
it makes him feel worthless, or even inhuman? Do you want this sort

of life for your child? If you've heard anything like this from your child, you've likely become jaded, frustrated, or even angry about school.

Anger is a double edged sword; it is an emotion that can either annihilate or protect you. It's a spiral, an emotion that can lead you downward into darkness, or inspire you upward into the light. Anger can be used to fuel your reactions to situations as they are or it can power positive action in working to change situations into what you imagine they might be. Feelings of frustration and anger about your child's education can be useful – *when harnessed as fuel for creating a positive outcome for your child.*

Perhaps until this very moment, the feelings of anger have just been a source of frustration for you. Today's the day that all that can change. As you get to know your child's learning preferences deeply, and how to make a choice to fit your child needs (the fuel), we'll create a spark to ignite that process for real.

In preparing to make changes for your child, I believe it's important that you know the full truth about school, because the truth has the potential to set you free. We'll talk about how to use your anger and frustration in a positive way, about how to channel the energy toward making a change for the better on behalf of your child. You'll come face to face with your own fears and begin to ask what sort of life you want for your child and what sort of parent you want to be.

While you may also have a noble heart that wants to see change for all children, the best wisdom I can offer you is to begin small. Start at home with your own child. The opportunity and wisdom you'll need to help others will come when you take care of your child's needs first. It's a lot like the preflight instruction lecture they give every time you board an airplane: *You must put on your own oxygen mask before helping the person next to you.*

So let's begin by defining *school,* or at least resurrecting the image of school as most of us remember it. If you are a parent or guardian of a child, it is likely that you went to school for 12 years. And as a product of the system of school, have you ever wondered:

- Why school is the way it is?
- Why classrooms are set up as they are?
- Why children are legally required to go to public schools for 180 days?
- Why attendance is compulsory for grades 1-12?
- Why kids are grouped by age (into grades) for learning?
- Who chose the content (curriculum) that children must master?
- Who created the specific order of curriculum and why?
- Why testing has become so much more important than actual learning?

Perhaps you have a sneaking suspicion that some of the answers to these questions are not as noble as we have been led to believe. We're going to tackle those questions and address some of your suspicions. You may feel a bit of annoyance and anger at some the answers, so we'll keep coming back to the notion that you will be most effective if you use those sentiments as the spark to make a positive change for your child, versus allowing the thoughts to derail you into complaint, bitterness, or shutting down completely. We'll uncover the truth so that you can fling open the cage door, setting you and your child free!

Step Back in Time

Whether you attended a public or private school, unless you were the product of tutoring, homeschooling or a progressive alternative, you know what school is like and how it works. Perhaps you remember a classroom where you sat in an individual desk while being directly instructed alongside 20 to 30 other kids your own age. You also may recall having a single teacher for all your subjects in the early grades, and then several subject area instructors as you moved into the upper grades.

Now think back to your fondest memories of school. Did they include PE, art, music, or recess? Were you a math or science lover? Perhaps you adored being read to by your teacher or the school's librarian. Did you look forward to field trips, taking trumpet lessons, or participating in a school play? Perhaps you recall the school lunches your mother packed for you or a visit from local business people on career day.

Isn't it interesting that for most of us, the most positive memories of school focus on things not directly related to learning specific curricular content?

Origins of School

The foundations of formalized education go back in the past a long way, prior to recorded history. For the purposes of our work together, however, we'll trace the roots of school, as we know it today in 2017, back to the foundation of the United States.

Do you recall what you were taught about the beginnings of our country after the Revolutionary War? Did you know that the founding fathers of the United States envisioned education as a way to cultivate all minds (think of their constitutional proposition that all men are created equal) toward an enlightened intelligence? Based on prior experiences in Europe, they intended a move away from vocational education of the masses, which added to the societal divisions they sought to erase, toward an era of intellectual enlightenment.

Does learning dedicated to enlightenment sound like the kind of schooling you remember? What about the kind of education your child is currently receiving? Do you consider yourself or your child intellectually enlightened by the education you received in school? Probably not. So what changed?

Thomas Jefferson, one of the signers of the Declaration of Independence, proposed that a strong local government was the best way to ensure freedom for all citizens. Even today, at least in theory, school is supposed to be guided by the federal and state government while falling under the direct control and responsibility of local government for its implementation. Our founding fathers' notion of a "free public education" is still a guaranteed right for all US citizens and remains a big draw for those who seek to immigrate.

The sad reality, though, is that most of what happens in school today is shaped by federal and state legislation versus remaining under local control. Instruction in school has changed, based upon the increasing influence of national standards and testing. Delivering the standards in neat and useable packages is the main reason that textbook companies and testing companies exist today. When textbooks are purchased by school districts, they often drive the creation of instructional curriculum to match. And so, much of what your child is taught comes from the outside influence of big corporations designed to present and test knowledge.

How and why did the state and federal government get so caught up in curriculum, standards, testing, and the evaluation of teachers? When and how did we lose our ability as parents to influence our children's education? In a nutshell, how did education go from being a locally directed enterprise to big business?

There are a couple of potential sources we can point to. This is at some peril, however, of becoming lost in a quagmire of loose threads and conspiracy theories. I'll briefly share some popular theories, but also caution you to take them lightly and to come up with your own conclusions. In the end, does it really matter why things have moved so far away from the ideal? Isn't it more important to recognize that there is a problem and to take action in the present moment than to worry about why there is a problem? Aren't you here to make changes for *your* child to in order to improve things now?

What Changed, Who Changed School?

If you really want to understand what's happened to our American educational system, you might spend months or even years reading the writings of various educational theorists and historians. And even then, you'd likely get confused, bored, or lost along the way. A shorter way to tackle the problem is to take a long, hard look at how things are now, identify the key issues, and then work backwards to uncover the sources of those problems, and the key players who created the megalithic educational system we now face.

Let's begin with a generalization, a supposition that education today functions more like the workplace than a place of learning. School operates more like a business, keeping our kids employed until they are 18 years old, than it does as an institution dedicated to promoting enlightened intelligence in the masses. For 180 days a year, most of our American students punch a time clock and do the bidding of their employers.

What does this description remind you of? A factory? Yes, very much so, and many writers have pointed to the similarities. They have used this metaphor to demand that schools and educators reform, evolving from an industrial model into something more progressive and appropriate for learners in today's information-based society. Reform has occurred in some schools, but it is not yet the norm.

Author John Taylor Gatto, in his book *The Underground History of American Education,* has speculated that the big system of school was primarily created to serve four of the major captains of industry at the turn of the 20th century: Andrew Carnegie, J. P. Morgan, J. D. Rockefeller, and Henry Ford. These men realized that creating a standardized, formalized, curriculum-driven system of education would be the best method for preparing the new workforce needed to run their factories most efficiently and profitably. The challenge today is that those foundations were laid several generations ago. We, as a collective society, have long forgotten the humble beginnings of school and their original purposes. We can no longer recall the beautiful dream offered of an enlightened and educated electorate. School has been co-opted by businesses motivated far more by the almighty dollar than by a sense of compassion for their fellow human man. Not only that, but our world today is rapidly changing from one of industry to one of information. The old model doesn't fit the needs of our changing society as well as it once did.

Many have called for reforms in education, and perhaps you've been one of those champions. I was one of those believers for a long time. I kept learning, changing, growing, experimenting, and trying my best to help make changes in the classrooms and schools where I worked. Over time, I became frustrated and angry with my inability to do what was best for my students. And so I finally decided to try to make change from outside the system.

I believe it's time to try some different tactics. For the most part, parents have lost track of the life that their children lead every day while at school. When our kids come home at the end of the day, they generally don't want to talk about what they've learned. Sometimes it's because they are angry, but for many it's because they are bored with it all and don't want to think about it anymore. They feel it's useless to talk about school, believing that there's no hope for change.

I can sympathize with today's kids' anger, having spent so many years in school. And I believe it's now unlikely that teachers and administrators will be able to change the system from within. The diffusion of responsibility for and the power over choices surrounding children's education have been delegated to invisible departments of education and companies. The path of influence has become virtually untraceable. There is so much content to be covered in a day, a week, a year, that it has become nearly impossible for most educators to do anything but put their nose to the grindstone and slave away. Talk to any school administrator about standards, testing, and curriculum and you may feel like you're talking to an overly full computer. New mandates continue to be added while little to nothing is taken away. And unfortunately, teachers have unknowingly become the progenitors of the very systems-based thinking they seek to free children from via an education.

I think it's high time we get back to the basics. To clean house. To lighten up. And to have some fun with learning again!

So now that we've recognized that school's function is to prepare workers for jobs from the past and that the curriculum taught is overseen by big business, what are we to do? What do we do with the knowledge that corporations and profit direct education far more than we were ever told?

First off, think back. It hasn't always been this way. We have historical precedent that points us to another way in thinking about education. The one-room schoolhouses of the past were primarily paid for by the towns in which they functioned. They functioned from a place of local control. If you've read about them, stories often focus upon the hardships of one teacher working to teach a vast range of children. Stories abound of strict teachers who boarded with various school families, and the antics of their students. What is often missed in these retellings are the stories of success. Few of the tales describe the children who learned the basics going on to become independent, free-thinking learners, other than a handful of famous change agents. It makes me wonder why.

Have you ever read about our 33rd present, Harry S. Truman, who is the most recent of our US presidents to have never earned a college degree? After graduating high school, Truman attended business college for a year, and later completed some coursework towards a law degree.

Like so many of today's children, Truman's love for learning was self-motivated and ultimately self-directed. He was a passionate reader and is reported to have walked miles to reach a library in order to check out books. His favorites were history-based, which appear to have served him well – certainly aiding his thinking and decision-making during his term as president at a time when things in the world were quite volatile.

Kids today are different. The world is different. And certainly, the future will be very different from what we see manifested before us today. Therefore it stands to reason that school will need to be different for your child in order for him to be successful. Instead of waiting for something to change, why not make a change for your child? You have the power to make things different for your child and this book will help you learn how to make your choices a reality.

Have you ever read Madeline L'Engle's book, *A Wrinkle in Time?* There is a particular scene where the three adventuring children come across other children on the planet Camazotz. Their first meeting takes place during the "hour of play," when they witness a boy bouncing a basketball and a girl jumping rope to an audible mechanical rhythm that seems to be coming from some unknown source. They come to learn that "IT," the brain-like entity that controls everyone's actions on the planet, is the source of everyone's synchronized movements and glassy stares.

Your child's hatred of school may well be a response to a feeling of being controlled in this manner. Changing class when the bell rings. Needing to seek permission to use the bathroom. Reading textbooks, taking tests, and doing homework. They may all feel like directed and mechanized movements to your child. Your explorations into who your child is, what he loves, and what he'd like school to feel like in the coming chapters will uncover the source of frustration – allowing answers to be found.

Chapter 3

Make It Stop Hurting!

"To sentence a man of true genius, to the drudgery of a school is to put a racehorse on a treadmill."
- Samuel Taylor Coleridge

I n Chapter 1, I shared some stories with you about my own journey through education and how I've come to be a passionate pursuant of what's best for kids when it comes to learning. While my own stories were those that demonstrated a bit of a positive spin, that's not to say I was without my own challenges. What those challenges taught me was to press on, to seek change, to try and help bring about the change.

Over the years I've been a part of the education of thousands of children and hundreds of adults. Along the way, I've met many interesting children. In my years in the public schools, there were many kids who didn't fit the mold, didn't like school, or didn't fit in, although many more children did find a place of refuge in the arts integration school where I taught for 17 years than might have in a more traditional setting. Having opportunities to make art, music, dance, and do theatrics was just the kind of motivation many kids needed to get the other "stuff" done. And so many difficult concepts were immediately clearer to kids when we approached them first by viewing a work of art or creating art as a way to measure learning.

Even though I got pretty good at making learning exciting and more interesting, I still felt overloaded by the size of my classes. I often found myself squeezing in content quickly in a uniform way because I felt I didn't have the time to know my students on a one-to-one basis. No matter how hard I tried, school became painful for me, and for my students. I became more distant and disconnected in my teaching, and my students knew it. What I didn't know back then but know now is that *it's absolutely critical to get to know a kid as an individual, to see him clearly, to hear what she is actually saying in order for learning to take place.*

In this chapter we are going to dig in deeply to get to know your child. To determine the source of pain. To help you prepare, and to help you know you aren't alone, I'd like to share some stories of real students I have known. They'll include how we figured out the child's pain point, and then how we determined a better fit for the child.

Jamie was a bright, beautiful, and highly intuitive young woman. She found it difficult to "fit in" with the kids in her suburban high school because of her lower socio-economic status and even more so because of her ability to see spirits. The day that she ducked under her desk when a ghost came charging at her during algebra class was a real turning point. At first her classmates just looked at her with curiosity. But when one boy put things together and taunted, "Another visit from your spirit friends, Jamie?" the teasing and bullying escalated. Within a week, Jamie began refusing to go to school in the morning. Then came numerous calls and meetings with administrators and teachers.

The school's counselors advised Jamie to stop talking about her intuitive skills. After a month of trying to "fit in," Jaime begged her parents to allow her to switch to a cyber school.

Jamie was assigned a full school course load, very similar to the subjects she'd been taking in her brick-and-mortar high school. She was able to finish out the last year and a half of her high school career with only a few minor bumps. Those mainly had to do with schedules and routines to make sure she got her work completed in a timely manner. Things really improved when she crafted a strategy to go to the local library at the same time every day to work on her courses. Jamie made time to do research on colleges, to locate scholarships, and to work on applications and essays. She also really loved being able to sleep in late and to take days off when she needed them. Jamie was able to graduate from her cyber high school at the same time as her former high school classmates and was enrolled in the college of her choice the next fall.

Perhaps you'll go the route Jamie and her parents did and make an actual change in the schooling format and location for your child. If you do, you'll need to make sure that the choices really fit your child and your lifestyle. You'll need to know what your child loves, how they learn, and what content matches your family values. There will be issues of location, cost, and the school's curricular focus, but those issues are secondary to your child's happiness and feeling of joy in learning. The day is long past where we can get away with the statement: I had to do it so you have to do it too. Today's kids are savvy. They know there are other options out there for them, and they deserve to find a place where they feel "at home" and good about learning and themselves.

It's critical that the choices you make are focused on not only what's best for you, but on what's best for your child as well. Sarah's mom and dad were separated and quickly heading toward divorce. Sarah's mom had moved to my hometown and wanted to put her daughter in the local school district. When Sarah's dad disagreed and wanted her to be schooled where he was living, the notion of homeschool came up. Because Sarah was in kindergarten, the transition was easy, and the judge agreed. There were few legal loopholes to jump through because kindergarten was still optional in the state.

Sarah's mom contacted the local district, gathered curricular guidelines for homeschooling, and filled their days together with creative exploration of early reading and math skills, combined with a lots of time for independent play. Sarah did end up going to a traditional school for first grade once her mom and dad's divorce and the custody judgment was final, and I believe that homeschooling with mom made the transition and life change of divorce more gentle. Sarah made the transition back to traditional schooling quite effortlessly, although there are days when she reminisces about the freedom she once had in kindergarten. Sarah is also an example of how choosing to try homeschooling doesn't have to be a permanent choice, and it doesn't always make a child incapable of returning to traditional schooling if necessary or desired someday.

Some of Sarah's story is related to understanding the laws in your state, and some of it is about knowing what you can and cannot do related to choosing an educational alternative. Later in the book, we'll talk more specifically about legal responsibilities, and where you can locate regulations to guide your choices around a different school or even homeschooling.

One of the biggest problems for most parents and kids today is feeling locked into the system of compulsory education. As though you must send your kid to school or you'll wind up paying fines, or even face jail time. There are intermediary steps in that process, and few parents actually wind up incarcerated. However, there are plenty of kids who walk away from school because of feeling that there are no other choices. Some end up in the juvenile detention system or worse. This book is about ensuring your child won't face any of those outcomes. There are other options out there, and together we will find the right one for you and your child.

Remember, your child's statement of "I hate school" is actually just code for "See me, hear me, listen to me and understand who I am." It's also a plea for you to ask questions about what isn't working, about what no longer feels good. And for so many kids, school actually feels like prison. So doesn't it seem strange that the system threatens children with going to an actual jail if they don't attend school? Isn't it strange that adults must coerce their kids to do something day after day that they hate? Why do we agree to send our kids to a job they hate? Do we do that to ourselves? That's certainly something to think about. But even if you are tied to work that you don't absolutely love, it's doubtful you'd be reading this book unless you sensed it's time to make a change for your child. If you are aware that your child is in trouble, you undoubtedly have a subconscious awareness of the power you possess to change your situation, and to live a life of your dreams. Even if you aren't able to change your own situation, you likely want a better life for your child.

It's time to let go of the old story so many of us tell ourselves. The one that says our kids have to go to school because we did. Or that it's just part of life to hate school because that's the way it is. It's time to stop spreading the lie that children will be a failure in life without school. It's time to look at the real truth, that many children wind up angry, bitter, or worse because of their experiences in school. It doesn't have to turn out like that. There are plenty of stories out there of people who had limited schooling, either by circumstance or choice, who went on to lead productive and even remarkable lives.

For example, if you do a search for successful people who either hated school, dropped out, or didn't finish high school/college and you'll uncover names such as:

- Presidents: George Washington, Abraham Lincoln, Harry Truman, Grover Cleveland, Zachary Taylor, and Andrew Johnson
- Astronaut: John Glenn
- Poets/Authors: Robert Frost, Mark Twain, Charles Dickens
- Nurse: Florence Nightingale
- Business Owners: Coco Chanel, Ray Kroc, Dave Thomas, Ralph Lauren, Bill Gates, Henry Ford, Andrew Carnegie, Steve Jobs
- TV: Oprah Winfrey, Ellen DeGeneres, Rachael Ray, Peter Jennings, Ted Turner

What does this list really tell us? That the shared global belief that school = success is not always true? Perhaps it's time for a new belief: that school *can* lead to success, and that school also can do more harm than good. Education and learning are what ultimately bring success in life, and they are not always a result of attending school.

There are so many stories of people who have achieved great things without completing the required 180 days, the prescribed curricular coursework, earning the highest of grades, or completing standardized tests. Quite to the contrary – many of the names on the list above found the greatest success outside of school, by charting their own learning path. They followed opportunity and their passions, learning just what they needed to know in just the right time in order to become a success.

So let's focus on what would really be your dream come true for your child. What do you want for your kid? Is it enough to just want him to quit complaining about school? Is it enough to want her to go to school, to get her work done? Most kids in the US attend school between 900-1000 hours a year (175-180 "days"), which works out to approximately 11,700 - 13,000 hours (2,275 - 2,340 "days") if they attend kindergarten through 12th grade.

Does it make sense to send your child off to a place they hate for such a large proportion of their young lives?

Let's assume that your real dream come true is something more like: "My child now loves learning," or "She absolutely adores her new school," or "He can't wait to get up in the morning start on his self-directed projects - he is learning 24/7!" From this point forward, we are going to work to stop pain, stop the fighting, and begin to identify ways to help your child flourish.

Chapter 4

Kids Are Different

"To be yourself in a world that is constantly trying to make you something else is the greatest accomplishment."
- Ralph Waldo Emerson, *Essays*

Now that we've tackled the questions about why kids have to go to school, why they may hate it, and what's wrong with the system, let's look more closely at kids themselves. With the prevalence of gaming systems, smartphones, tablets and laptops, today's kids are more wired than ever before. Their lives and thinking are constantly being shaped by the media channels that they are exposed to day in and day out. Before we attempt to make any changes to the outside reality your kid faces in school, we need to better understand the interior landscape of today's child. They are very different, but how?

How Are Kids Different?

As an elementary teacher I began to notice changes in my students approximately 15 years ago. They appeared to have differences in their ability to pay attention as well as a changed ability to grasp and retain the content that I had been teaching for many years. Like so many teachers, I first looked at these changes as problematic – as the student's "fault." Then one day it hit me. I was the teacher, I was 100% responsible for learning. If my students weren't "getting it" or "retaining it," then I needed to understand why, figure out what would work better, and change what I was doing to help them succeed.

At one point I had an opportunity to have my students take a learning styles assessment, and I was surprised by the results. The four classic learning styles that teachers are introduced to include:

- visual (those who learn best by seeing)
- auditory (those who learn best by listening)
- tactile (those who learn best through touching)
- kinesthetic (those who learn best through doing and moving)

I had taken the assessment myself and learned that my preferences were for visual as well as tactile learning activities. The majority of my students, however, preferred tactile and/or kinesthetic learning opportunities. My students were totally different than me! I also recognized I had been tending to teach in styles that I was most comfortable with as a learner. Meaning, I was teaching in a manner which didn't match my students' needs. OUCH. Working in an "arts-integration" school (a school that utilizes art, music, dance, and theater to enhance students' learning outcomes), I was lucky and able to change fairly easily to accommodate my kids. I had many opportunities to offer students experiences with works of art, to make art, and for my students to learn through tactile and kinesthetic experiences.

When I left the K-12 learning setting, I dove more deeply into studying the topic, curious if others were noticing the differences and changing their teaching methods. My explorations uncovered a growing movement toward seeing the change in learning styles as a gift vs. a curse, as so many teachers lament. While not the norm, many more teachers today offer students a chance to learn in ways that honor all four learning styles, capitalizing on the excitement generated when addressing a favored style and offering supports to strengthen the weaker skills.

ADD / ADHD

If your child is having difficulty in school, it's possible that someone has mentioned the terms Attention Deficit Disorder (ADD) and Attention Deficit Hyperactivity Disorder (ADHD). For those less familiar with the acronyms, here's a brief primer. ADD is now considered an outdated term. ADHD, the more common term used today, is defined as a brain disorder that can include inattention, hyperactive-impulsive tendencies, or a combination of the two.

In the late 60s, the American Psychological Association (APA) formally recognized the existence of both ADD and ADHD. Although there was some discussion of a child's inability to pay attention in the psychological literature as early as the 1900s, the first medications to treat the two disorders were discovered between 1930 and 1950. The Centers for Disease Control (CDC) reported that between 2012 and 2014, 14% of boys and 5.2% of girls between the ages of 5-17 had been diagnosed with the condition. Statistically those numbers mean that ADHD affects, on average, 10.2% of all kids. Some researchers consider the rise in diagnoses to be of an epidemic proportion.

There's lots of speculation about why ADHD diagnoses are on the rise. Some believe it's because we are more aware of the condition and therefore more able to diagnose it. Others speculate it's a function of a pressure to over-diagnose by the medical and pharmaceutical industries.

A third set of beliefs center around recent changes in the American diet. Specifically these proposed influences center around increased access to processed foods, decrease in consumption of fresh fruits and veggies, and an increased exposure to toxins and chemicals in the environment.

The rise of diagnoses is alarming, as is the increase in prescription of medication as the solution. Research on the long-term effects of ADHD medications is just becoming available. The main drug prescribed today is Ritalin, a stimulant, which actually has a reverse effect on young children. With a similar chemical composition to cocaine, some of the side effects of Ritalin include anxiety, insomnia, dizziness, headache, increased heart rate and/or blood pressure, and occasionally psychosis. Couple that knowledge with the results from early studies showing that there is a potential for brain damage in young adults who have taken the drug for years, and a growing trend in young adults to continue to use Ritalin into adulthood as a "legal" stimulant. So what's a parent to do?

There is a growing trend toward seeing ADHD as the "new normal." That is, many researchers and writers propose that we begin to consider ADHD as new adaptation in our species vs. a deficit. They suggest that the behaviors diagnosed as maladapted are actually skills we should instead celebrate! This shift in thinking doesn't always align well with the structures in place in our schools. One of the main reasons behind the push to medicate children is to make them more capable of fitting in at school. More able to fit in with peers in overloaded, overcrowded classrooms, more capable of following a teacher's directions.

A growing number of parents are refusing to medicate their children. Instead, they are asking for accommodations to be made to meet their child's different needs. Where and when this is not possible, many parents are making the choice to move their child into a different educational setting.

If you want more information about ADD, ADHD, and the ways in which you can work with your child at home and in school, check out

Attention Deficit Disorder: A Different Perception, by Thom Hartman. Thom not only traces the origins of the "deficit" back in time, he clearly outlines the ways in which we can see the disorder as a *needed skill* in our changing society. He touches on the ways in which we all can begin to celebrate these evolutionary changes in our children in order to maximize their time and effort spent on learning. You might also enjoy Chris Mercogliano's *Teaching the Restless: One School's Remarkable No-Ritalin Approach to Helping Children Learn and Succeed.*

Indigo, Crystal, and Rainbow Kids

Another set of terms being used to reference the differences seen in kids today are: indigo, crystal, and rainbow. Considered by many to be a pseudo-scientific term, "indigo child" comes out of New Age philosophy. It describes a set of children who possess special, unusual, and occasionally supernatural skills. The terms crystal and rainbow have come along as well to further describe kids who seem to present a different level of knowingness than the average population of kids. It's fairly common that children in these three categories wind up with an ADD or ADHD diagnosis as well when they reach school age.

Many describe indigo, crystal, and rainbow children as having come into the world with a level of knowingness directly related to their purpose in it. These kids sometimes act with a level of entitlement or with a high level of confidence in sharing who they are with anyone that will listen. Sometimes indigo kids have difficulty with or are frustrated by the adults who assert authority over them. They are most frustrated when direct authority is applied without an explanation. Indigos appear to gravitate toward free thinking and creative thought, often possessing the ability to see different or better ways of doing things. These children feel free to speak their minds and they often do!

If you resonate with the notion of indigo, crystal, and rainbow children and would like to know more, there are some excellent resources available. To learn how you can support the home life, diet, schooling, and career path of an indigo child, check out both *The Indigo Children* and *The Indigo Children: Ten Years Later,* by Lee Carroll and Jan Tober. A shorter read is *The Crystal Children*, by Dr. Doreen Virtue. And you and your child might enjoy watching *Indigos* or the documentary *Indigo Evolution.* Both movies are currently available to stream online.

Going Beyond Categories/Labels

As I have read authors who focus on how kids are different and *specially-abled* vs. different and *disabled,* my thinking has dramatically changed. I realize that the system of school isn't designed to play to these kids' strengths. Indigo, crystal and rainbow kids are truly different, so why are we trying to force them to fit into a system that doesn't feel good to them? If we are truly caring adults, it's up to us to learn more about these kids, and to create opportunities for learning that best fit who they are. Author PMH Atwater proposes that we drop the labels all together. She suggests we should just assume that all kids are different, notice what their strengths and weakness are, and then play to their strengths. I couldn't agree more!

Atwater has identified some of the strengths that today's kids demonstrate as:

- a tremendous intelligence, perhaps "genius," even when failing in school
- extreme creativity in areas such as music, art, technology, inventing, and innovation
- intuitive, psychic, or healing skills
- a group-oriented preference, excellent problem-solving ability, and excellent cooperative, volunteer, or humanitarian skills
- demonstrating quirky, unusual, or abstract ideas for a kid their age

Some of the weaknesses Atwater has identified include:

- impulsivity, overconfidence, easy to anger, and little tolerance for deception
- sensitivity to food, drugs, chemicals, various types of energy fields
- a preference for mentors vs. authority figures
- an expectation that things will come easily (some see this as laziness)
- a lack of boundaries
- a fear of silence

If your curiosity has been piqued by these two lists and you want to know more, I recommend *Children of the Fifth World*, by PMH Atwater. Buyer beware. This book is an in-depth and comprehensive look at the evolution of today's children. It also offers a predictive look at how today's rapidly changing society will be impacted by these new kids and vice versa. Once you read her works your thinking about kids and schools will likely be changed forever! PMH is the author of additional books on "the new children" that can be easily located online.

Does Staying in School Make Sense?

At this point you may well find yourself wanting to get your kid out of school tomorrow. It may make sense, based what we've learned so far about the purpose of school, why it isn't working, and how children are different. But before you take the leap, I'd ask you to consider advocating for your child. Why? Because school could still be the right place for your child, and you just might facilitate change for all kids by speaking up.

How do you do that? Well, the first step to falling back in love with school is to know that it's an inside job. You won't fix the outside system of school by going in with guns drawn, ready to take down a teacher that you believe has made your kid hate school. Advocacy will require some looking inside of yourself and getting to know your kid inside and out well. Once you have a better picture of who your kid is, and have made peace with the fact that school isn't serving your kid's needs, you will be able to approach the school calmly, asking for what your child needs to thrive. Requesting changes for your child in a calm and logical manner has the best likelihood of being acted upon by your child's teachers. If your child's teacher feels as though you've come to help them better serve your child, you may well be able to help make changes right from inside of the school. And then, if you are met with defensiveness, indifference, or an unwillingness to collaborate, you'll have good reason to change plans.

There is a logical process to figuring this all out, by the way. In the next five chapters we'll explore steps you can to take in order to tackle the issues in ways that will transform your child. The steps will not only help you to decide how to proceed, they'll offer methods for helping to change your child's thinking about school. The steps in sequence are:

- Know Your Child (from the inside out)
- Identify Options (sort through and simplify the options available)
- Make a Choice (choosing the best option for your child)
- Creating the Space (setting your child up for success)
- Get Going! (taking action with and for your child)

You can't make mistakes; you can just make choices. What all my years in education have taught me is this: We learn far more from the things we do than from the things we read about. We learn more from watching our parents than from listening to what they say. Yes, you are sitting and reading this book. But unless you use it to propel yourself to take action for and with your child, it's unlikely anything will change. As Mahatma Gandhi once said, "Freedom is not worth having if it does not include the freedom to make mistakes." Ultimately, we are after your child's freedom to learn, grow, and thrive in this world. It's inevitable that you may make a few mistakes along the way, but take heart, you can't ruin your child by changing his educational setting.

Have you ever heard people refer to certain young children as "old souls"? I've met a few of these kids who seem to possess a wisdom beyond their years. One of them was a little boy, about two years old, whom I nicknamed "Little Bear" because of his propensity to crawl around and growl like a bear. When I greeted him the first time, Little Bear looked at me and said, "I hate you." I was surprised. I stopped, quieted myself, and responded, "I love you. Do you want me to go away?" He replied again, "I hate you." To which I said, "Well, I love you!" This went on for a few minutes with us bantering back and forth, I love you, I hate you, I love you, I hate you.

Later, when I had a chance to talk with Little Bear's mom she told me it was a new thing. Perhaps it was just a fluke, perhaps he was just in a sort of "parrot" stage, or he was enamored with hearing adults offer love in response to his use of the word hate. I doubt he was thinking much about it at age two.

Weeks later I was thinking about the whole situation and I had a realization. By saying, "I hate you" in his cute, little-boy voice, Little Bear gave me an opportunity to counter the statement with love. It was a profound gift. He was providing me with a physical reminder to respond to hatred with love. By practicing that skill with a toddler, I was also strengthening my ability to be loving with difficult adults in my life. Now on days when I feel the "I hate you" energy coming from some person in my life, I often reflect back on Little Bear and find it's easier to respond with "I love you" energy.

Why am I sharing the story of Little Bear with you? Well, I believe there are more and more of these kids in the world today. Many are old souls who are here to teach us adults a thing or two. While these old souls may possess ancient knowledge worth listening to, we, as the mature adults, are responsible for guiding them with the wisdom we've gained through the living of our own lives. I hope that the road ahead, learning how to be a wise guide to your child, will be fun and delightful!

Chapter 5

Knowing Your Child

"A human being has so many skins inside,
covering the depths of the heart.
We know so many things, but we don't know ourselves!
Why, thirty or forty skins or hides, as thick and hard as an ox's
or bear's, cover the soul. Go into your own ground and learn to
know yourself there."

- Meister Eckhart

So far we've tackled how and why school may not be serving your kid as a unique individual. We've also looked at the ways in which school may see your kid through using labels. We've noted how those labels may be overlooking gifts hidden just beneath the surface.

Spiritual teachers such as Serge King, Wayne Dyer, and Mike Dooley have shared ancient wisdom that states *our thoughts create our reality*. Translated into more conventional terms, the teachings point out that if we focus on the negative, we'll get more of that in our lives. And the converse, that we will generate more positive results by seeing the opportunities in a situation. The teachings point to a simple truth about learning: that *you have a better chance of making change in learners' lives by focusing on their gifts than by blaming or shaming them into compliance*. By focusing on your child as differently-abled, as having gifts to uncover, we will begin to explore and identify your child's talents, preferences, and needs.

My friends Kim and Dan have been involved in spiritual studies for most of their adult lives. Their son Kileigh (Ki for short) has accompanied them to workshops, meetings, and gatherings while still in the womb. And nowadays, Ki is seen as part of the group. In fact, in most of the circles his parents attend, Ki is honored as the child's voice in decision-making processes.

Kim recently shared a story about having Ki's chakras read. A healer had looked at the boy's energy systems and offered information about the color, shape, and spin of each chakra, along with a diagnosis. When Kim and I chatted about the diagnosis, I wondered out loud, "Yeah, but what does that mean?"

Having the diagnosis of what was out of balance with Ki's chakras was certainly interesting, but I wondered what the three of them had done with the information. Had they done any healing work, made any changes in their environment, or talked about doing anything differently? Kim indicated that they'd looked at the information together with Ki, but that nothing more had come of it.

I'm sharing Ki's story because, in the coming exercises, I will ask you to gather some information from your child and to use it to change what is no longer working. If you haven't done so already, it's a great idea to start a journal and to take notes while you read this book, especially as you and your child work through the following exercises. Keeping track of your thoughts and your child's responses will help you to create a clearer picture of who your child is today, what might benefit his growth and development, and how to craft a plan for the future.

But what's more important is that you actually *do something* with the information you gather. Talk with your child about the information and get clarity on what the responses really tell you about yourself and your child. You'll likely need to make changes to what you are currently doing, to directly address the issues and challenges you see come up as you work through the remainder of this book. It's not enough to simply be aware; awareness is simply the first step. Nothing will change unless you actively address the identified problem.

You might consider talking with your child about this book. Let your child know that you've realized there is a problem at school and that you are learning more about how to address the issues. Share with your child that the first part of making any challenging situation better is to first understand the problem more clearly. Explain to your child that you want to know more about who they are as a learner, what they like, what they don't like, what's working, and what is not, so that you can help adjust the problem areas. You may also let your child know that this process will be a chance for the two of you to spend more time together and to get to know each other at a deeper level.

Exercise #1

Let's begin with some basic questions you might ask your child after this first conversation: What do you do during the school day? How does each particular activity make you feel? Here's an easy outline you can use to help your child identify what school is really like, with some sample responses to get you going:

What I do in school:	How it makes me feel:
Ex: I sit in a chair for man hours, only able to get up when I raise my hand.	Ex: <u>Frustrated</u>: My body feels stiff and achy. It makes me feel like I'm a slave or in prison, that I can't take care of my own body.
Ex: I take a Spelling test every Friday, a Math test every Monday, Science and Social Studies tests are always on different days.	Ex: <u>Stressed</u>: My heart races and I sometimes feel dizzy. I feel like I'm being tested all the time and that is the only thing teachers care about.
Ex: I got to the art room once a week and get to paint, draw and use clay.	Ex: <u>Happy</u>: My body is usually bouncy and excited. I love art class, I love working with my hands and making something beautiful to look at.
Ex: I have sustained silent reading time after recess every day.	Ex: <u>Creative</u>: My body becomes peaceful and relaxed. I look forward to this time to go inside my imagination and see the characters.

Experiences vs. Emotions & Feelings Exercise (sample)

You'll notice that the above examples include both positive and negative experiences. Consider making two copies of the empty chart below, or copy it into your journal and ask your child to fill out one with the positive and one with the negative experiences they've had in school. This will help you to begin to see some patterns, to compare what your child does like and what he doesn't. You may even decide to complete a set of two charts for yourself, thinking back to your own school experiences. Having a dialogue with your child about what school was like for you is a potentially powerful way to connect. Be careful, however, not to focus too much on your past experiences with school or your own painful memories. Our main goal is to attend to the needs of your child and to help make positive changes related to school as quickly as we can.

What I do in school:	How it makes me feel:

Experiences vs. Feelings & Emotions Exercise

Look over the two charts your child has created and notice if the feeling words she has chosen are emotional ones or if they describe the physical sensations she feels in her body. This is an important distinction to make in understanding how she is experiencing school. We often use the word "feelings" to mean both physical sensations as well as our emotional states. While similar, the two are actually different functions of the human brain.

Here's a quick definition of emotions and feelings to clarify the distinction:

<u>Emotions</u>: are instinctive or intuitive states of mind that are influenced by circumstance, interaction with others, and mood. Emotions sometimes create sensation in the physical body in response to outside stimulus, which can help identify the state.

<u>Feelings</u>: are the brain's interpretation of the emotions, and are often colored by past experiences and beliefs.

Emotions and feelings work both ways – emotions in the body can trigger feeling responses, and just thinking about feelings around a particular situation can trigger an emotional state in the body. For example, my friend Shannon's son Ben is an outgoing and gregarious seven-year-old. He knows nearly all of the adults in the small town where he lives by name, and is confident in greeting them with a handshake and direct eye contact. In school, however, his desk is placed facing a wall, away from other kids. Ben often reports tightness in his stomach, feeling ill, and feeling angry and upset. Occasionally this leads to Ben's mom keeping him home from school or having to pick him up early.

There's a lot going on in Ben's story, as I'm sure you can imagine. It's pretty easy as outsiders to see the teacher's mistake in forcing an extroverted boy into a desk that isolates him from his peers. It's an obvious contradiction to who Ben is and what he needs to feel good about himself. Both physical and emotional responses are activated in him when he is isolated from classmates. And when Ben begins to think about going to school, he sometimes revisits the isolation as his stomach begins to tighten. This leads him to feeling angry, tense, and unwilling to get on the bus some mornings. Ben's challenges are not isolated. For many children, this sort of situation becomes a downward spiral unless attention is brought to the emotions and feelings and their source is uncovered and attended to. Honoring and supporting who each child is in the classroom setting creates a relief valve.

Exercise #2

The first relief valve we can create for your child is to clearly identify and name the feelings he is having related to school. To do this, we will use a scale that I've adapted from the work of my book coach, Angela Lauria, to identify the intensity. This will help us order and rank feelings and issues that are occurring at school. Then we will introduce your child to some strategies for coping with those feelings no matter when or where they occur. One of the outcomes of learning to identify feelings and tend to them is that your child may actually begin to enjoy school. Another benefit is that you will be collecting clear evidence of what's going on in order to facilitate a change in the school setting for your child. It's the sort of information you can share with teachers and administrators.

Our goal with this exercise is to help your child identify their feelings about school, rate those feelings' intensity, and then learn ways to change the intensity level – especially if the feelings are not at a level that is comfortable. The scale we'll use runs from a -10 to a +10, with 0 being neutral. Feelings at the +10 level might include excitement about going to school, loving classes or classmates, feeling in the flow with learning, etc. Feelings at the -10 level might include physical symptoms such as vomiting, headache, nausea, or feelings of fear or intense anxiety. At the 0 or neutral level, your child might experience a blasé attitude about school, neither caring if he goes or not, sometimes stating, "Who cares."

School Feeling Scale

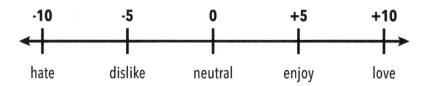

Take some time to share the scale with your child and discuss it. It might be useful to make a copy of the scale on a large piece of paper, adding in other feeling words to describe different states and experiences.

When I shared the scale with Kileigh recently, he had some great insights about how parents might use the scale to determine urgency in changing school settings. He felt that with each particular level, a parent might consider:

- +5 to +10 – no change is needed
- 0 to +5 – that the child might be able to suggest a change for himself
- -5 to 0 – suggesting a change for the child
- -10 to -5 – that this is an urgent situation, requiring a triage-like focus

Now let's use the chart to get more specific and hone in on the key triggers for your child. Ask your child to help you better understand the elements of school that relate to each end of the scale. For instance, you might talk about the school feeling scale related to the following influences:

- Day of the week (ex: Mondays vs. Fridays)
- Time of day (ex: morning, midday, afternoon, dismissal)
- Specific teachers or classmates (ex: Mrs. ABC, or the class bully)
- Methods of learning (ex: direct instruction, worksheets, homework, projects, group-work, oral presentations)
- Subject areas (ex: reading, math, science, social studies, foreign language, etc.)
- Learning environment (ex: classroom, computer lab, library, home, etc.)

- Particular materials (ex: books, audios, videos, computers, hands-on materials)

Are there additional areas you can think of to discuss? Great! What's important is that you make notes of your child's responses, or even record them on the chart itself. Pay close attention to the things that wind up on the extreme ends of the scale. These are your child's points of greatest pain and moments of greatest pleasure.

Helping your child both recognize and balance the scale is a step toward increasing his ability to be okay with school. It's also a great way to gather information about your child's likes and dislikes should you decide to go another route with school. These details will help you find a school that better fits your child's strengths and passions vs. aggravating his dislikes and weaknesses. You can use also this scale with your child anytime he or she is having a concern or intense feeling about school by simply asking where they are on the scale. From that point forward, you'll be able help improve the feeling.

One way to tackle intense negative feelings about school is to revisit positive experiences that have occurred in school in the past. Together, you can visualize the items related to school that fall on the positive end of the scale. Recreate memories of those happier times in school together with your child either out loud, in the mind, or through some form of artwork. Helping your child imagine a better situation in the moment can help bring a level of relief from negative feelings. It's also a great strategy for your child to use when in school and facing challenging emotions and feelings.

Another way to work with the scale is to look at the items sitting on the -10 end of the scale as teachers, or lessons, to be explored. If your child is able, probe a bit deeper to see if you can determine the source of negativity for each item. Perhaps it's a recent event that has been hidden and requires attention, or an action on the part of the teacher.

For example, your child may have a hatred of recess because he is being physically assaulted by a classmate. Or perhaps it's the memory of a past experience with a subject area that is recreating the negative feeling state. For example, your child may hate weekly spelling tests because of a low grade on one test weeks ago. Knowing the source of an emotion can help your child begin to recognize that memories exist in the past.

To probe more deeply you might ask your child, "Is there another way to see this situation?" Or you might ask, "Is this feeling really true? How do you know it's true?" To help your child shift the feeling state away from past experiences you can ask: "How would things be different if this weren't true?" or "Can you imagine the opposite of this situation?" So much of our actual experience of situations comes from the way we look at the situation and the feelings that are created from that viewpoint. Sometimes just changing the way we look at a situation improves the actual situation in dramatic ways.

Lao Tzu, the ancient Chinese philosopher, once said: "If you are depressed, you are living in the past. If you are anxious, you are living in the future. If you are at peace, you are living in the present." Our goal is to begin to help your child recognize where his thoughts come from – past, present, or future – and to help him begin to live in present-moment awareness.

My friend Jessica recently sold all of the family's assets, including their home, car, and much of the furniture, in order to purchase land to build a new business. The land requires lots of TLC as it was recently timbered. Jessica and her partner Jay spend much of their time on the land, working from sunup to sundown, clearing away the brush and stumps that remain. Wyatt and Dean, Jessica's two sons, are often required to come along. For many months, the boys hung out around the campfire playing games on their tablets or throwing rocks. In an effort to get them active and involved in the creation of the new family business, mom often took away the tablets and required the boys to work on creating trails on the land. Wyatt began to hate being out on the property and eventually refused to help. After trying several ways to involve him in other aspects of the business, Wyatt's mom decided to drop the subject and quit asking for help.

A few weeks ago I had a chance to visit with Wyatt and his mom on the land. Wyatt took another young boy on a walk down one of the trails to see a stream on the property. When I caught up with them I was totally stunned to hear Wyatt teaching the younger boy all about the rock formations, how to find particular mineral deposits, and how to navigate the stream now covered with leaves. I asked him what had changed his feelings about being on the land and participating in the family business. His response was simple. He had realized his own tendency to tune out when on his tablet. He had also noticed the comfort, relaxation, and connection he felt when being outdoors on the land. Wyatt had noticed his thoughts, noticed how they made him feel, and had chosen to see things differently. His lived experience was transformed by his change in thinking. What had once felt like drudgery to him, helping out on the land, had now become fun and relaxing because of his change in thinking!

Exercise #3

Next we will gather some detailed information about your child's specific experiences in school. This time we'll look through the lens of "content knowledge" – the subject areas your child is required to learn in school. We'll do this in order to find out where your child's interests and passions lie.

Doing the things we like or love is a lot like food; it helps to fuel us, but in a different way. Where our physical body requires calories to survive, our mental and spiritual selves require a different source of nourishment. Making sure that your child gets in a "daily dose" of the things he loves is a great way to help build his ability to attend to the more challenging things that feel difficult or hard. Below, work with your child to list all the subject areas she takes in school according to how she feels about them.

School Subject Categories

Hate	Indifferent	Like	Love

Now review the completed chart with your child. What do you both notice? Is there a balance between what he loves to do and what he dislikes? Did she list most subjects in the "indifferent" category? Or do most of the subjects land in the "hate" category? Talk about the patterns you notice and think about what that tells you both about your child's relationship with school.

To take this activity one step further, choose a subject from your child's *love* category, or some outside activity that your child particularly loves to engage in if all subjects fall in the indifferent or hate categories. Start off by talking about the subject. Then ask your child to draw a picture about it, or collaborate to write a brief description about it. You may want to include details such as:

- a title and summary of the subject
- where the activity falls on the feeling scale
- why you like the subject
- describe the teacher who teaches it
- how you feel about the teacher
- what kind of things you get to do in the class
- why you like doing those things
- what activities you do related to this subject at home (because you want to)
- do you always love this class? Why or why not?

Another way to see the challenges your child has with school is to recognize its cycles. For many kids, the love/hate relationship with school fluctuates much like the seasons and weather. Some of that can be attributed to the fact that our system of education is still based on an old agrarian model. Just as the seasons bring to mind various stereotypical activities, school has its own predictable patterns.

Fall is usually seen as back-to-school season, and focuses on setting rules, creating routines, getting to know one another, and getting started with content learning. Many children may look forward to this time of year with excitement, while others avoid thinking about school until the last minute. Where some kids relish the new classroom, new teacher, and new classmates, others hate the perceived waste of time doing the same old icebreaker activities year after year with different teachers. A friend recently told me the story of his all-out panic in August the summer before his fourth grade year. He had forgotten how to do long division and was terrified to go back to school without this skill set. No matter the student, fall is a time of tremendous emotion for children when it comes to school.

Winter is one of the busiest time in schools. It's hunker down and work time. Winter is the season when most content is taught. Your child may enjoy this rapid, no-nonsense focus on learning, or she may buckle under the pressure. And the promise of vacation breaks help some students make it through the rough patches, while for others they create brief moments of freedom from school that make it even harder to return when they are over.

Spring brings one of the most intense times in school as it often includes standardized testing. It's the time when instruction often moves away from freedom and creativity, and focuses in on test-taking strategies or coverage of tested content. I don't know many kids who enjoy this time of year, although there are some natural-born test lovers out there! This intense focus on testing has actually created a whole movement behind the notion of "Opting Out." If your child experiences fear or anxiety around testing, some research on the movement and your rights as a parent can help you to decide whether or not to have your child continue to participate in standardized testing. Many administrators will try to convince you to reconsider a choice to opt out, however, only you know what's best for your child.

Summer. Sweet summer vacation. Many children think of this season with fondness and great anticipation. A time to be free and to do what you want. A time to be idle, to swim, to read, to travel, and to play. For others summer can be a time of boredom, or of hunger, without the support of school lunches. Summer can also prove a challenging time for parents, work-wise, with children's need for supervision.

Optional Activity

Another way to get to know your child and what interests him in regards to learning is to take a day to play hooky with your child. I only recommend doing this if truancy or attendance are not a critical issue with your child.

Talk with your child about the fact that learning happens everywhere, all the time. Ask your child what they'd like to do if they could take a day to learn in their own way. Perhaps they'd choose to go to the library, the zoo, or a museum. Do choose something that will have a learning focus to it, and plan out how you'll use the day. Start with how you'll begin the morning – perhaps making breakfast together and packing lunches. Focus on when you'll leave, how long you'll stay, and when you'll return home. If possible, visit a website to plan out maps, time frames, costs, etc. Have your child keep a notebook or draw pictures of what she sees along the way. When you return home, work together to create some sort of summary of your adventure.

This, in a nutshell, is what homeschooling families do every day. While most do not go out on field trips every day, most do take time to plan out learning for the day and to share what they've learned at the end of the day. Pay close attention to your child's level of enjoyment in this sort of activity. It will give you clues about what sort of educational setting is the best fit.

You now have an idea about what works and what does not work for your child. You also know how various aspects of school create a love/hate feeling in your child. You've taken time to categorize subject areas even further. Have you started to notice any patterns?

Exercise #4

In your journal or on a separate sheet of paper, write a summary about what you've learned so far. Your child, if old enough, can write about it too – or he can draw a picture to show what he's learned in talking with you about school. In your summary describe:

- my child's favorite/least favorite subjects are:
- the things at school that trigger positive/negative emotions/ feelings are:
- my child would say the best/worst parts of school are:
- the best/worst time of the day for my child is:
- at school my child would like more/less of:
- my child talks positively/negatively about these teachers and kids:
- if my child could do anything he wanted all day long it would be:

Hang onto this summary – it's going to be a useful tool for the steps you choose to take next. In the next chapter we are going to discuss the options open to you going forward. They will include three progressively complex but completely doable choices:

- transform your child's current school
- choose a different school for your child
- transform your child's learning life

Earlier in the book, I shared that my friend called me a "child whisperer." Throughout this chapter I've shown you some of the strategies I use to get to know kids deeply. Everywhere I go, I meet kids who seem to sparkle. That is, they are energized by the things they are doing or by sharing their interests and passions with me. What I've come to understand is that being able to be fully present with a child creates the connection and the trust that allows them to share their deepest calling.

Most often the kids I meet don't actually know what they want to do with their lives yet, but they can tell me or show me what they love. Doing what you love is a guidepost along the path of a life well-lived. Hopefully the activities you've completed together are already helping you to develop a deep knowing of who your child is.

Much of what we've been doing in these activities is to bring mindful awareness to your child's experience of school. Mindfulness is a term that has become more well-known in the past few years. Stemming from ancient eastern practices of yoga and meditation, mindfulness is the intentional paying attention to thoughts and feelings. Its purpose is to bring awareness to our feelings and emotions in order to mindfully choose how to respond vs. reacting. With young children, so much of their action stems from reaction, as opposed to thinking things through. While this book is not primarily about mindful practices, I highly recommend you check out some of the great books on mindful parenting. Beginning to teach your child some of the self-regulation skills that are inherent to mindfulness will allow you to begin to help your child bring peace to the difficult moments he or she has identified in the previous exercise.

School is something we were all taught we had to do, and often we believed that we had to suffer through school no matter what. We were taught that without a good education, we'd be a failure in life. Hopefully you now can see that those are just beliefs we, as a society, have chosen to believe. School can be a place of joyful learning, and oftentimes it is not. You now have a deeper understanding of your child's experience at school, what's working and what is not. And it's time to take action to create some change for your child, based on what your child has been asking for all along by saying, "I hate school!"

Chapter 6

Identifying the Options

"It's so much easier to suggest solutions when you don't know too much about the problem."

- Malcolm Forbes

N ow we will take a look at the wide variety of educational options available today. You likely already have some ideas. Perhaps you have heard from other parents about a local magnet or private school. Having spent so many years as a student, and then many more as a teacher in the big system of public education, I am no longer convinced that a neighborhood school is the best choice for every child. While I do see many children who love and thrive in school, my own two nephews being prime examples, I see many more who do not.

In my personal work beyond my coaching and mentoring, I also collaborate with small groups of concerned parents to create new schools for today's kids. I'm a big supporter of parents who choose alternative schools and those who choose to homeschool. I am here to support you fully in your decision-making process no matter the choices you make. So let's begin.

Exercise #1

To set the stage for looking at educational alternatives, we need to return to the notion of finding the best fit for your child. Let's focus on your child once more. Take a moment to relax and take a few deep breaths. Once you are both relaxed, ask your child to close his or her eyes and imagine the very best day of school EVER! Allow your child to take time to explore the scene for as long as possible. If she needs some encouragement, you might ask questions such as: Where are you? What are you doing? Who else is there? What can you see, hear, smell, taste, touch? How do you feel?

As your child begins to share what she is seeing, take notes, and most importantly, try not to interrupt. Alternatively, if your child is younger or just simply prefers to write or draw, offer that option as well. Be sure to add the answers you collect to the journal you have started.

When I've done this activity with kids, they always have the most amazing answers. Sometimes they focus on things such as wearing pajamas, eating popcorn, and watching movies. Other kids focus on time spent outside in nature, building and exploring. And some, believe it or not, focus on content areas they love – most often asking to spend independent time with deep questions they have that have gone unexplored so far.

It's interesting. When I've done this exercise with parents and children present in the same room, it presents the greatest challenge for adults. Many adults focus on the joyful experiences they would like to see available to their child. For others, the exercise brings up painful memories of school and a deep need to make sure that their children do not face similar challenges. If the exercise brings up deep emotions for you, take time on your own to unpack the memories. It's important as you work to improve school for your child that you recognize the experiences you've had that might inadvertently hamper your efforts.

Exercise #2

I'd like you to make a prediction. What sort of school setting do you think would work best for your kid based on what you've learned about her so far? Do you think he'd like to stay in a big school with lots of friends? Prefer a smaller school where she is known by all the staff and students? Would he prefer being with kids his own age, or would a multi-age group work better? Would she like to attend a school with a specific focus or theme? Would he prefer a school in the city, or a school out in nature? Would your child like to take classes online? Or would he love to be at home or doing his school work by your side? Write about what you think your child might like in your journal. We'll come back to this after the next section to see if your predictions were correct.

As we touched on earlier, education in the US is compulsory. That means, in the strictest of terms, your child is required by law to attend a public or state-accredited private school for a specific number of days. While the length of the school year varies from state to state, more and more states are requiring attendance for 180 days from grades K-12, or until the child reaches age 18 or graduates from high school. The options available to parents today are far more diverse than ever before. From public brick-and-mortar schools to charters, private schools, online cyber schools, and homeschooling, there is a form of education to fit the needs of just about everyone.

Option 1: Transform Your Child's Current School

Now that you know your child and his preferences regarding school better, would it possible for him to stay in his current school with some changes in the classroom? This choice has some obvious benefits. It allows you to maintain the routines you and your child are used to. And it generally requires the smallest number of sacrifices to be made, both time-wise and financially. And it also allows you to begin to transform the learning space for other children as well.

However, choosing to transform your child's current school requires taking direct action on behalf of your child. You've gathered lots of information about your child in working through the exercises together. This is all useful data to share with your child's teacher and possibly the school's administrator. It will allow you to advocate and ask for precisely the modifications your child needs to be happier and more productive in school. Staying with your current school will also require monitoring your child's emotional state at home as well as discussing progress with your child's teacher. We'll touch on some action steps to take in the next chapter if you believe Option 1 would work best for your child.

Option 2: Choose a New School

There are some valid reasons to consider changing the school that your child attends. Most importantly, changing schools can ultimately help you locate a setting where your child will develop a lifelong love of learning. We'll take a look beyond your current school – be it the neighborhood school, a local private school, or a charter school – to locate all of the options in your area. The number of choices available today is vast, so we'll break your choices down into some broad categories to help you narrow down what works best for you.

Public vs. Private

Brick-and-mortar schools can be generally placed into one of two categories, public or private. Those point to the source of funding behind the creation, maintenance, and "flavor" or focus that a school adopts. Public schools receive funding through taxes, most often a portion of local real estate taxes. A public school uses curriculum (the content that your child is expected to learn at a particular grade level) guided by the standards (what your child should know and be able to do at each level) to instruct children. Currently in the US, 42 out of 50 states have adopted the "Common Core Standards." Each state has the freedom to choose how and when to adopt the standards. Some states adopted them early, others have rejected them completely, while a few states switched somewhere along the way.

There is a fairly heated national debate around the original purpose of the Common Core Standards and their current impact upon teaching, learning, and testing. Originally intended to create some uniformity across schools nationwide to ensure equal opportunity for growth and consistency for kids when moving from state to state, a growing number of opponents now question their true purpose. Big issues being debated include increasingly narrowed topics of study, increased teaching to the test, and obvious ties to the big business of textbooks and standardized assessment. To learn more about the debate and to weigh in if you are so inclined, you can search the Internet for more information about the Common Core.

As you consider the differences between a public or private choice for your child, you'll want keep curriculum and standards in mind as they determine much of what your child will do during the day. You can locate information about curriculum and standards used on a school's website or by asking questions of the school's administrator. The main differences you'll find between public and private schools are the cost and the focus of the curriculum. Private schools generally charge tuition, and have more freedom to design their curriculum around the priorities parents find important. While some private or parochial schools do use the Common Core, many do not. Because they are funded through taxes, public schools utilize the state-adopted standards to guide the creation of their curriculum.

Private Schools

If you are interested in exploring private school options, there are three basic categories to consider: religious, alternative, and traditional. Below is a list of potential options for each category:

- *Religious:* Christian, Friends (Quaker), Islamic, Jewish Day, Mennonite/Amish, Protestant, and Roman Catholic
- *Traditional:* Academy, All-girls, All-boys, Boarding, College Prep, International Baccalaureate, and Military
- *Alternative:* Democratic, Free, Montessori, Open, Progressive, Reggio Amelia, Sudbury, and Waldorf

In choosing a private school, consider the kind of learning your child has expressed an interest in. What kind of environment or learning opportunities might she enjoy? Many families choose a religious school in order to include faith-based instruction as part of the school day, which is not found in public schools because of legislation requiring a separation between church and state. Traditional private schools often provide students with a more rigorous college-preparatory focus, an opportunity to learn in a single-sex setting, or to receive military training during the school day. Alternative schools are often the most diverse option available, providing students with opportunities to learn in a more open, independent, and self-directed manner.

A Focus on Alternatives

Democratic, Sudbury, and *Free schools* are perhaps the most relaxed and child-focused of all schools. Allowing students the freedom to decide when and what to learn, most utilize a formal democratic process, which directly involves students in all aspects of the governing and functioning of the school.

Montessori schools feature mixed-age classrooms that allow for individual independence and freedom to learn and grow using a discovery model. Students approach learning through the use of materials vs. through direct instruction. Montessori schools generally employ educators who have been trained specifically in the schools' unique methodology. Most Montessori schools focus on primary-aged children, with middle and high school students either returning to public schools or attending other private school options.

Reggio Amelia schools base their curriculum on principles of community, responsibility, and respect. Students follow a self-guided curriculum to learn through exploration and discovery. Begun in Italy after WWII, the schools see students as apprentices to learning, as opposed to being the target of direct instruction.

Waldorf schools focus on imagination, working to build artistic, practical, and intellectual skills in students. Their philosophy is based upon the writings of Rudolf Steiner, the founder of the anthroposophy movement in Germany. With thousands of schools globally, Waldorf schools are one of the most common independent school options.

To learn more about these various types of schools, you may choose to search for a particular type of school or do a general search to see which options currently exist in your area. For a comprehensive guide on the subject of alternative schools, consider *The Parent's Guide to Alternatives in Education,* by Ronald E. Koetzsch, Ph. D. The Alternative Education Resource Organization (AERO) also maintains a list of many new and innovative alternatives across the globe. Be sure to check out their website for the interactive map and links to some of the best alternative education resources on the web at www.educationrevolution.org.

Charter Schools

In the realm of public schools, many states have created a "school choice" option, better known as charter schools. A charter school is a publicly funded school, usually run independently from the local school district in which it is located. Rather than drawing students from its attendance area like a public school, charters draw their student population from applicants in a wide variety of ways. Currently, 43 states and the District of Columbia offer charter school options (Kentucky, Montana, Nebraska, North Dakota, South Dakota, Vermont, and West Virginia currently do not permit charter schools.)

Like a public school, charters are required to follow curriculum and standards set forth by the state in which they are located. Charters often are created with a special theme or teaching methodology in mind, and so they are one option for locating a creative match for your child when you're unwilling or unable to pay for a private school. Some charter schools are actually launched by parents or teachers in a community with a keen interest in offering unique options for kids.

An increasing number of charter schools are being opened and operated by corporate entities, so it's good to take a look at the school's charter before you decide. The data on the success rate of charter schools is mixed. Many provide unique opportunities for children to excel academically, while many actually have lower performance rates than their traditional public counterparts. Academic performance is only one way to understand your child's success in school, though. Good grades and high test scores on standardized examinations have long been considered the best predictor of a student's success in later life. This belief is beginning to shift, however. Consider our earlier list of folks who never graduated high school and went on to successful careers. A growing number of colleges no longer require SAT or ACT scores for admissions, and actually encourage the submission of portfolios or writing samples as a better indicator of a student's success in higher education. This points to the need for you to take many things into consideration when guiding learning options to support your child's later success in life.

As you begin to sift through the school options in your area, you'll likely come across websites that sort and rank schools by many of these academic measures. You'll need to decide if that's what is most important to you. If not, you can refer back to your description of your child to consider which criteria matter most and look for the school that fits your child's specific needs.

Online/Cyber Schools

As correspondence schools have grown and matured into Internet-based coursework, cyber schools have become a viable option for learning to take place outside of the confines of the traditional classroom. Growing at a rapid rate since their birth in the 1990s, cyber connects students directly to content and teachers via the Internet. Today, a wide range of cyber programs can be found online. They include independent schools, cyber charters, and homeschool resource centers. It's even possible to find cyber programs located within traditional schools. In such schools, students are enrolled in online coursework with the option to take the classes from home or in a traditional classroom while maintaining access to extracurricular activities.

Your mileage may vary with cyber schools. Find out as much as you can about the source of the content taught by each cyber as well as the credentials of the educators. Many cyber schools purchase their curriculum from another source, so what may seem to be a different option for your child may actually be a replica of another program. Some cyber schools have created their teaching curriculum by simply cutting and pasting readings and assignments from textbooks into an online course management system. If your child did not enjoy reading and responding to textbooks in his brick-and-mortar school, then this type of cyber would provide little to no relief from the misery. If he enjoyed working with textbooks or would prefer to move more quickly at his own pace, then a cyber could be a good choice. There are some more original and authentic choices out there, so take some time to look around. Just as there are websites that feature reviews of schools based on academic success, you should be able to locate the same information for the cyber of your choice.

Moving

Have you ever considered moving to a new town that has an amazing educational opportunity for your child? While certainly a big decision that involves the whole family, there are plenty of parents who relocate so that their child can study a high-level sport or develop a talent or skill on location with a well-known expert. Cases in point: Olympic hopefuls who move to have access to a world-renowned coach, or the child actor whose family moves to Hollywood. If your child has a passion that they hope to cultivate into a lifelong career, big changes in location and educational setting may be in order for your family.

Option 3: Transforming Your Child's Learning Life

As you learned in the previous section, cyber schools are one of the options you can take advantage of should you decide that learning outside of the brick-and-mortar school is the best fit for your child. Cyber and other pre-packaged curricula are a way to bring learning into your home without the need to create daily lesson plans for your child from scratch. And there are lots of options out there. A simple search on homeschooling will turn up websites that offer lesson plans, workbooks, worksheets, ideas, and resources, either for free or a fee. Do keep an eye out for the site's focus, as some are dedicated to religious homeschooling, while others are hands-on experiential-based or even more general in nature.

One of the myths about homeschooling is that it's just "doing school" at home. On the contrary, homeschooling can be a totally transformative activity. Traditional teachers are classically trained to offer a standardized curriculum to 25 or more children at a time, and that has a big part to do with why textbooks and curriculum are created. And uniform lessons are intended to make learning more manageable with standardized materials. Homeschooling parents sometimes adopt traditional materials in order to feel more comfortable making the transition from school to home, to help their child adjust, or simply because they do not know there are other options. As you've likely discovered, your child is a unique individual and deserves to have an opportunity to learn the things that interest him or her. Homeschooling is a fantastic way to offer that kind of freedom.

Taking a leap into homeschooling can feel strange or even downright scary. One great way get your feet wet is to watch Jeremy Stuart and Dustin Woodward's documentary, *Class Dismissed*. It's the story of one family's adventures leaving school and settling in on a learning model that works best for the two daughters. It's an honest look at the ups and downs of the process, including the need some kids have to "deprogram" their mindset, finding routines that work, and tackling what to do when a child decides they want to return to school.

Free Range Learning: How Homeschooling Changes Everything, by Laura Grace Weldon, is a useful book to reference if homeschooling is feeling like a possible fit for your child. It covers topics such as where learning takes place, the importance of play, connecting with others, and nurturing your child as a learner. Weldon includes rich examples and suggestions for adding in adventures, field trips and time spent in nature, as well as unique ways for tackling the subject areas of math, PE, the arts, language, history, and ethics through the recruitment of outside experts and mentors for your child.

As you begin to learn more about homeschooling, you may want to locate homeschooling groups or cooperatives in your area. If none exist locally, it's worth considering starting one on behalf of your child. Cooperatives create the time and space for homeschool children to collaborate with other kids and their families. They typically meet weekly in order to share resources, develop friendships, and support one another with unfamiliar curriculum. Some cooperatives operate free of cost, while others charge small tuition fees to cover the cost of classes or the use of a shared learning space.

Another term you may come across while considering homeschool is the term *unschooling*. It describes the activities supported by a growing number of parents who have chosen to make self-directed, personalized, and unstructured learning a part of their child's everyday life. Based on the understanding that we all start out as young children hardwired to learn, unschooling capitalizes upon a kid's natural interests and passions; learning happens as a byproduct of those explorations. While homeschooling may or may not follow a particular curriculum, unschooling generally does not.

You may be wondering if unschooling is legal. As a form of homeschooling, it is legal to unschool your child. If the idea interests you, there are a growing number of unschooling websites and blogs to guide you through the legalities and particulars. You might also enjoy listening to teenager Logan LePlant describe his *hack-schooling* experiences in a TedX talk from the University of Nevada.

The main thing to keep in mind is that homeschooling, unschooling, and hack-schooling all face legal requirements for reporting. To determine what your requirements are, search the web, call your local school district, or visit the Homeschool Legal Defense Association (HSLDA) at hslda.org. Check in with other homeschooling parents in your area and you'll learn many tips and tricks on documenting your child's progress in order to satisfy state or district reporting requirements. In many cases, reporting can be as simple as keeping a three-ring binder with categories, filling in each area with examples of projects and work along the way.

In the next chapter, we'll focus in on making a choice *with* your child vs. *for* your child. We'll take a look at choosing and moving forward with the heart in mind as well as the head. Finding the best fit for your child is a personal blend that can include:

- keeping things your child loves about school
- working to eliminating things your child hates about school
- staying in the same school
- selecting a new school
- choosing cyber education, homeschool, or even
- making it up as you go along as an unschooler or hack-schooler

Making a change can seem daunting. And sometimes the thought of leaving school can seem like a recipe for failure. Not so. Take the story of Walter Russell. Born in Boston in 1871, Walter only went to school until the age of ten. He took a job at a small store to help make ends meet for his family, continuing learning on his own. Walter raised enough money to send himself to art school and began a career painting children's portraits. Following his interests and passions, he went on to develop cooperative real estate for artists in New York City while living above Carnegie Hall. He taught himself the art of sculpture, and eventually developed the University of Science and Philosophy in Virginia, an early correspondence school. A quick search will uncover lots of information about Walter's various publications and his diverse and impressive achievements.

One of Walter Russell's core beliefs and teachings was that we all have the capacity to tap into the genius of the universe, to solve any problem, and to learn or do anything we set our minds to. I believe the same is true for your child!

The next step in the process is to make a choice. And you need not wait until the end of the school year to make a change for your child. Both the cyber and homeschool options can be put into place within a week or two after notifying your local school of a change and enrolling in a curricular program. The choice between making a change immediately vs. waiting until the end of the school year should be based upon the intensity of your child's hatred of school, and how soon you want to see a change in your child's emotional state.

Chapter 7

Making a Choice

"It is our choices that show what we truly are, far more than our abilities."

- J. K. Rowling, *Harry Potter and the Chamber of Secrets*

In the last chapter, we looked at the three main ways to directly address your child's dislike of school: Asking for changes to be made at your child's school, locating a different school that better fits who your child is and how she learns best, and finding options for learning outside of a brick-and-mortar building. In this chapter, we'll tackle how to wade through all the information and make a choice. You'll then craft a plan for implementation and put the wheels into motion on behalf of your child!

If you're feeling any anxiety or fear in this moment, stop and take a deep breath. You're heading out into the unknown. The anxiety you may be feeling is likely coming from not knowing or being able to see what lies ahead for you and your child. This fear may also be coming from remembering the past. In both cases, the emotions may potentially thwart forward progress.

What's most important in this moment is that you make a choice for your child and implement it. If the new option you select still isn't the best fit for your child, you can always try another option. Like most parents, you'll want to try and get it perfect the first time out. Don't worry about that. Fear of making a mistake will only keep you from trying something out. The most loving thing you can possibly do for your child in this moment is to move forward with a change, demonstrating to your child that you have seen and heard her needs loud and clear. And that you are willing to do whatever it takes to make things better for him.

On Transforming Your Child's Current School

At this point you've done lots of work to get to know your child and to know more about what school is like for him day in and day out. You know the specifics of what does and does not work. Now it's time to address the issues that came up with the adults who are responsible for educating your child, creating the learning environment, teaching the content, and so on.

Think back. What were the biggest aggravations your child described? Make a short list of the biggest issues. Each of them will determine who you will talk to and how to handle the conversation. Was the biggest issue your child's teacher? Relationships with other students? The content/curriculum? Time or pacing? Classroom size? A need for more movement or creativity? Something else?

You might begin by talking with other parents. The point is not to gather ammunition to attack the teacher, but rather to discover if the problems are isolated to just your child. If the problems your child describes are limited his experience, then you can jump right into sharing what you've learned about your child and ask for some accommodations to be made. Generally begin by talking with your child's teacher. Going over a teacher to speak with the administrator can make the entire situation more difficult, creating a teacher who is far more reluctant or even unwilling to work with you. Think to a time when someone shared issues they were having with you with a second party – and the information got back to you. How did it make you feel? Did it make you want to work to resolve the issues with that person? Didn't you wish she had just come and talked to you up front, even though the issues were uncomfortable?

If you've decided to meet with your child's teacher, some advance planning is in order. Choose a day and time when you will be able to devote your full attention to the conversation. It's probably best to meet before or after school when the teacher won't be as preoccupied with upcoming classes and students. If possible, plan to meet at the school in your child's classroom, so that you can get an even clearer idea of what your child is experiencing day in and day out. This is especially important if you've not had a chance to visit the classroom before. Next, create a list of questions you'd like to ask the teacher. Focus on asking broad questions that address the core issues your child has been having. For instance, if your child reports being bored doing worksheets every day, ask the teacher to show you the kinds of work that kids engage in during the day. If your child has issues with a bully, ask what the teacher has noticed in regards to your child's interactions with classmates. If your child reports a need to be more engaged physically or creatively, ask questions about how often she is offered gym, music, art, or other project-based activities. There are lots of good guides to parent/teacher conference questions and techniques on the Internet that can also help you come up with your own list of questions.

Be sure to bring your journal to keep track of your questions and to write down items as you go along. Listen to the teacher carefully and try to make some eye contact. In order to have your child's teacher work with you as a partner, aim to help her feel comfortable and that you are an ally. Getting defensive will tend to undermine the conversation, so you may want to think ahead of time about how you'll handle the situation if your child's teacher projects any frustrations by accusing your child of being the problem. Even if your child has been displaying some sort of inappropriate behavior, it's the teacher's job to help create a resolution to the problem in collaboration with you as the parent. Blame on either side prolongs a child's suffering and does little to determine solutions.

So how did the meeting with your child's teacher go? Well? That's awesome! Perhaps you've found a way to make school fit better for your child. All it may take to continue to improve your child's opinions of school is to maintain conversation about what's working and what isn't, and to continue sharing that wisdom with your child's teacher.

Did the meeting wind up being less productive than you'd hoped? Then it may be time to step up the game. Going to talk to the school's administrator (principal) should generally be your last course of action. But if you've met with your child's teacher and made no headway, or you've come to an agreement about changes that can be made to support your child and things haven't gotten better after a few weeks, it might help to talk with the school principal.

The same rules of thumb you practiced in meeting with your child's teacher apply to talking with the school's administrator. Focus primarily on the information you've gathered about your child and what he needs, talk about the meetings you've had with the teacher as positively as you can, and speak generally about the changes you hope to see for your child.

Do your best to come across as clear and confident, as a calm advocate for your child's highest good. Complaining about your child's teacher, the school, the district, etc. will likely go nowhere with an administrator – they hear complaints all day long. Unless your child's teacher is completely incompetent, it's more than likely that the building administrator will recommend continuing to try to make changes in the classroom. If you are not okay with that, consider asking for the administrator to change your child's class if the option has not come up already. Sometimes a change of teacher can actually make a huge difference.

So how did the meeting with the administrator go? Is there a plan in place to help support the needs of your child? Is the situation improving? Is your child beginning to enjoy going to school? If you're unhappy with the results of these additional meetings, or the plans created to support your child's particular needs don't seem to be happening or making a difference in your child's attitude, it may be time to move on to Option 2.

On Choosing a New School

If you have met with your child's teacher or administrator and have not been successful in creating an inviting educational environment for your child, it's time to consider trying out a new school. Perhaps you've jumped ahead to this option because of all of new things you've learned about your child that indicate a different learning setting would be a better fit. It's also possible that the situation in your child's school is so negative or dangerous, that you know it's time to take matters into your own hands. Regardless of how you've come to this point, I commend your courage in seeking out a new school. The process is not as hard as you think it might be, and there are folks out there like me who can help you make decisions, should you need a guiding hand.

So what kind of school would entice your child, would be enjoyable, even fun? Think back to the previous chapter. What sort of learning environments described piqued your interest? A public school nearby, a charter with a particular theme focus, a smaller private school, a boarding school, a cyber school? Now is the time to dig in on the Internet to see what alternative choices exist in your area, or to locate a school that matches your child's specific needs.

There are several ways to begin. Search locally to see what's available within driving distance, or search globally for the specific type of school you're interested in. The search terms "school finder" and your geographic location will usually turn up a variety of options as well as websites that list and rank schools in your area. If you already know that an alternative would suit your child best, you might start with the AERO website at www.educationrevolution.org and use the "find a school" tab as your starting point.

Remember the story of my friend Jamie and her need to find an alternative to her neighborhood high school? Jamie's parents knew that they weren't able to pay for a private school, there were no other suitable charter high schools available in the area, and they recognized that they weren't comfortable directing her education on their own. They decided that a cyber school was the best option available, so they began their search using the term "cyber school" and the name of their state.

In Jamie's state, there were several accredited online schools to choose from. As a family, they took some time to read about them, to make a list of the pros and cons of each, and to dig into the online comments made by parents and students about each school. Jamie and her parents were also able to schedule a visit to several of the cyber schools with local offices or learning centers. Some cyber schools now offer face-to-face support for students when needed alongside virtual meeting spaces. Together, Jamie and her parents selected the school with the attributes they felt best addressed her strong desire to attend college. The cyber staff and teachers were supportive and responsive, getting her up and working in her new online courses within a few weeks. If you choose to go the route of changing schools to a local brick-and-mortar option, you'll need to contact your child's school to determine the application and transfer process, and you'll need to take timelines into consideration. In some cases, schools (especially the more exclusive private ones) have strict deadlines for enrollment. Many require an application and payment in February to secure attendance for the next school year. So timing will be of critical importance and might necessitate your child staying put in his current school longer than he'd like if you select a school with enrollment deadlines.

If your district requires written notification of your child's change in schools, you can find great examples of a withdrawal or transfer letter online. Sometimes your local district will even provide a template of the document for you. The most important item to keep in mind is timelines. Once you sign your child out of school to participate in another educational setting, the clock will start ticking. Your state will specify the time you have to either enroll in a new school or to commence your plan of action for homeschooling. Keeping an eye on the timelines will help to avoid the consequences related to truancy.

On Changing Your Child's Learning Life

Thousands of families are making the choice to transform the experience of education for their children by homeschooling or unschooling their children. In simplest terms, homeschooling your child means that you as the parent are taking back responsibility for the learning of your child. While you may feel some fear or trepidation about this choice, you are actually in good company. Schooling from home, which until recently was seen as strange or unusual, is rapidly becoming mainstream. In 2016, there are upwards of 2.3 million children registered as homeschoolers in the United States alone. How can so many parents and kids be wrong?

You may be thinking, yeah that sounds great, but homeschooling is just an option for…

- families with one spouse making a large income, allowing the other parent to stay home and teach the kids
- children whose parents have college degrees or teaching experience and who know how to teach their kids
- families with a desire to focus on religious training
- kids who are antisocial, ill, or have specific athletic or creative aspirations

While some of the above statements are true, many more families are choosing homeschooling for the freedom it provides parents to:

- accelerate/decelerate academic coursework to match their child's abilities
- try learning approaches not available in traditional schools (e.g., learning outdoors or while traveling with their parents)
- allow the child to learn while participating in and learning about the parent's work (e.g., on the farm, in the workplace, or alongside a parent's home-based enterprise)
- provide flexibility in scheduling, and freedom to interact with adult mentors or experts in the child's area of interest
- provide increased safety and freedom from peer pressures related to bullying, alcohol, drugs, violence, sexuality, etc.

You might be wondering how you'll tackle homeschooling. There are a broad number of options available to you. Those can run the spectrum from "unschooling" to a setup similar to traditional schooling in your home. Unschooling offers your child the most freedom to explore his or her own interests, and requires the parent to have an understanding of school district reporting requirements – documenting and filing evidence during the year for submission at the year-end review. More traditional models of homeschooling offer pre-packaged curriculum options, guides, and checklists, providing you with the materials you'll need to guide your child's learning. A search will reveal plenty of options, both paid and free, which can help you to set up a plan for your child that will ensure that learning takes place while satisfying legal requirements.

Whether you purchase online courses and materials or paper-and-pencil guides, remember to consider locating a local homeschooling group. New ones pop up every day, and they are a great way to share the homeschooling task with other likeminded parents. While traditional schooling segregates your child to an age-specific group, homeschooling offers your child a chance to learn from and with kids in a broader age range. It's a great way for your older child to learn to lead and nurture younger children, or for your younger child to be stretched by the abilities and interests shared by older kids.

In the case of my friend Michelle, choosing an alternative for her son Delyn took more time, as he had received an autistic diagnosis from his traditional elementary school and faced challenges with limited attention span too. Michelle researched the local laws governing alternative education and homeschooling and determined that the best option was to sign Delyn out and teach him herself. She visited the local school district to meet with the administrator responsible for directing homeschooling families. Michelle was coached on what she'd need to gather during the year to document her instruction of Delyn and how he had mastered the required curricular content during the year.

To help keep track of Delyn's progress, Michelle organized a three-ring binder to gather work samples. She included each of the content areas, and she crafted a cover sheet that listed all of the items Delyn could include as evidence of learning. She also created a daily routine to ensure that Delyn completed his traditional curricular materials every morning, allowing him to explore topics of interest on his own when finished. Because they were living in a remote wooded area, Delyn had time to learn a wide variety of outdoor skills from a nearby neighbor. Michelle and Delyn documented his learning in a variety of ways, through writing, drawing, and even photos. They chose to gather hard copies of his learning outcomes, but many other students and parents accomplish the same task using digital tools and by creating a digital portfolio.

One of the interesting outcomes reported by Michelle and Delyn, as well as most homeschool families, is the abundance of extra time available each day. What takes students and teachers approximately six to seven hours to complete in school often takes the homeschooled child only two to four hours. *This can be every kid's dream and a parent's biggest nightmare.* Without a plan in place for channeling your child's newfound freedom as an opportunity to investigate, you may find yourself putting out fires. With a little bit of organizing with your child, this new freedom to explore can lead to exponential growth in your child!

We'll cover the topic of planning out the learning day in the next chapter to ensure that your decision to homeschool your child is a success. We'll also talk about how to set up a dedicated learning space and gather resources to help make your child's learning activities both focused and fun!

We all have heard the old saying that "kids learn more from what we do than from what we say." It's profound wisdom. My friend Shannon's son Ben is an exemplar, at the ripe old age of seven, of the power of learning alongside a free-spirited parent. Shannon runs a local farmer's market and also sits on the town council in their small town. The last time I popped into the local coffee shop for a visit, Ben sat with us for a few minutes, fully engaged in the adult conversation about micro-schools and independent learning. At one point he got up quietly and walked over to another table of adults, joining in on their conversation. Ben knows just about everyone in town, and most folks talk about how he'll likely be the town's mayor someday. In fact, the current mayor has even made jokes about Ben's communication skills being so strong that he could easily recruit his own militia to take over the town government before his 18th birthday! Ben has gained much of his passion and confidence in communication from watching his mother interact and collaborate with adults.

Homeschooling your child has tremendous potential for allowing your child to thrive by your side. Your child has a rare opportunity to see how you navigate your responsibilities. And if you work from home, he will see how you negotiate, collaborate, organize, plan, and thrive, all while helping him to connect academic studies with the practice of daily life.

If you've gotten to know your child and what works best, the entire process can be tackled in just a few weeks. Choosing the best option for your child can feel overwhelming, but there is help out there. You can hire an educational coach to work you through the steps of the process!

Chapter 8

Creating the Space

"Life isn't about finding yourself, it's about creating yourself."
- **George Bernard Shaw**

Whether you've decided stay put, to change schools, or to strike out on your own with homeschooling, creating a dedicated space for learning in your home is a powerful practice. Not only does it provide your child with a place that's comfortable and inviting for doing school work and homework, it sets the tone that *learning is important, that learning is valued*. Remember, what's most important to us gets most of our attention. In our fast-paced world, so many of us sit and work on our laptop wherever we wind up. While that method is great for getting ourselves motivated and getting things done on the fly, it isn't always the best idea for long-term success where learning is concerned.

Early on in her transition out of the local high school, Jamie identified the need to create a dedicated learning space as she began her cyber school classes. Her challenges began with her family's unfamiliarity with online learning and the need to set and maintain a steady schedule. Her mom and dad both had high school educations and worked a variety of odd jobs. Dad was responsible for tending to a public garden space next to the house while mom did house cleaning and taught cosmetology part time. Both of Jamie's parents operated from organic schedules that shifted according to the season and availability of work. Neither of her parents had any prior experience setting up a learning space or the knowledge of how to monitor and ensure that Jamie was getting her work done on time.

Jamie had received clear guidelines from her cyber school about how often to be online, when to meet with teachers virtually, and when to submit weekly assignments. Because her home environment lacked a dedicated learning space and motivation to get the work done in an efficient manner, Jamie started to fall behind. After a few weeks of Jamie missing deadlines, we sat down to talk about strategies to support her need for structure in order to get her work done more efficiently.

We started by looking around the house for a place to create a dedicated space for her learning to occur. With three younger siblings and a number of family pets, the house was usually in a happy state of cluttered chaos. The setting had clearly provided her with ample distractions up to this point, so we decided to pay a visit to the local library to see if it might be a better fit. Because Jamie already had her driver's license and had purchased a used car, she had the ability to get herself up and to the library each day to complete her school work.

Once we determined that the library was open seven days a week, we crafted a plan for Jamie to go to the library from 10 am until 2pm on weekdays, and then to make up any days she missed on Saturday or Sunday. Jamie loved the opportunity to sleep in the extra few hours each morning while her peers were already in high school. Not only was she able easily complete her weekly work during the daily four-hour sessions, she had the added benefit of quick access to materials needed to complete many of her assignments. Jamie also got to know the librarians and even took advantage of workshops offered to support college applications, scholarships, and student loans applications offered at the library. For Jamie, setting up her learning space at the local library was a win-win situation in so many ways!

Now take some time to look around your own home. Is there an appropriate space that can be dedicated to serve your child's learning? Lots of families choose an extra bedroom to double as a classroom, add a desk and bookshelves to the child's bedroom, repurpose a well-lit hall closet, or even transform a traditional dining room into classroom space. The latter is especially popular with families who have several children being homeschooled at the same time. If you have a home office, perhaps there is a corner where your child can work by your side during the day. No matter where you choose to set up your child for learning, collaborate with your child in determining the furniture, lighting, and equipment they might enjoy, and that also fit your budget.

If setting your child up at home or choosing to have your child work at the local library aren't options, there are other possibilities available outside of the home. Many homeschool and online cyber students now complete their work in a local coffee shop. My friend Becky's teenage daughter Rose drops in to the local coffee shop when her mom goes to town. She sits at one of the high-top tables overlooking the baristas and either works on her online coursework or reads quietly while her mom runs errands. Becky knows the manager, who fully supports and endorses the needs of many local homeschoolers as both customers and friends. In fact, once a week, the local homeschool co-op meets at the same coffee shop to work together while each child has their weekly violin lessons at the nearby music center. Recently, the coffee shop manager has starting tutoring Rose in Social Studies, to supplement deficits in the online curriculum. You might also be able to take advantage of a local homeschool cooperative's drop-in center or workspace.

A fairly new option to investigate are co-working or shared working spaces. Designed for home-based entrepreneurs and singleton professionals to have access to workspace, technologies, and meeting spaces, they can be found in many cities. Some operate on a fee-per-use basis while others charge a reoccurring monthly membership fee. These co-working spaces are often bright, cheerful, and stylish, and many include access to coffee, food, larger meeting/boardrooms, and even video gaming spaces. The benefits of shared working space include the opportunity for your child to experience a work atmosphere while having access business owners who may potentially serve as mentors. Check your local area for this type of space and ask to see if they'd be open to allowing your child to use their space for learning purposes.

Even more "out there" are the kids who complete all of their learning while traveling the country with their parents in an RV. Some of these families are dedicated to adventuring and touring full-time, while others travel in order to support the working needs of one or both of the parents. Either way, this particular lifestyle provides children with access to a perpetual field trip in addition to meaningful, place-based content learning. You can find out more about this gypsy lifestyle by searching online using terms such as road schooling, nomadic homeschooling, or learning on the road. You'll find lots of great stories and inspirational information, including dates and locations for group meet-ups with other families who are out learning on the road.

Have you located the perfect place for your child to learn? The next step is to create a plan for the learning. Like my friend Jamie did, you'll want to think about the hours best suited to your child's learning style. Three to four hours are generally more than enough for a child to complete a homeschooling or cyber curriculum each day. This will leave a number of hours free in which your child can plan to do any number of self-selected activities. By planning out the day together, you can ensure that your child is on task and focused while you are engaged in other activities around the home, be they homemaking tasks or your own business enterprises.

I have some friends who have adopted a "two hour" method to plan out their learning week. Using this method has brought them together as a family. Each member creates a chart for the upcoming week on Sunday afternoon and then all of the charts are posted on the refrigerator so that everyone knows what's on everyone else's agenda. They created a simple spreadsheet with GoogleDocs and then blocked out their common hours for sleep and shared meals. The rest of the blocks of times are open for each individual's selections. Color coding makes it easy to see if an activity is something being done as an individual, or in community with others. Have a look at the sample below for inspiration and then try creating a scheduling chart for you and your own child. Enjoy!

	Sun	Mon	Tues	Wed	Thur	Fri	Sat
12:00am	Sleeping						
2:00am							
4:00am							
6:00am							
8:00am	Shower/ Breakfast						
10:00am	Family Outing	Online Classes					Family Activity
12:00pm							
2:00pm		Lunch/ Recess					
4:00pm		Independent Projects					
6:00pm	Dinner/ Family Game						
8:00pm	Quiet Reading						
10:00pm							

ME Color	WE Color	Group Color	Other Color

Each student crafts 2-hour slots for work, rest, play, and family time. It could be adapted to 1-hour slots if desired

The Question of Technology

Let's face it. Technology is everywhere and many kids are exposed to digital input from the moment they are born. And here's the thing. A growing number of studies indicate that technology is changing us, rewiring our brains – and not always in ways that are improvements. In beginning to think about your child's learning environment, you will undoubtedly need to deeply contemplate the role that technology will play.

Some of the best examples I've seen in mindful parenting with technology actually come from my close circle of family and friends. My brother-in-law Brian works for one of the planet's major technology security providers. He and my younger sister Betsy both work from home and do nearly all of their work remotely using the best of today's digital technologies. My nephew Liam, however, has been given access to technology at home slowly and in intentional, pre-planned doses. When I visit with the three of them, I'm always pleased to be able to engage in adult conversation with Liam, not needing to cajole him to put down a device first. His mom and dad have made family time a priority, and consequently meals around the table with them are filled with lively discussions about current global topics, sports, school, and creativity! Difficult topics about politics and global crises are also a big part of our conversations, and Liam's thoughts and input are always welcomed and encouraged by everyone.

My friend Michael, who works for "that super popular Internet search engine company" and is the single dad of three young boys, has his own unique ways of encouraging creative thinking beyond the digital screen. Screen time for the boys is limited to the weekend and non-school nights, and then only after chores are finished. Digital books are offered more freely and are read and discussed together, while video games and Internet surfing are monitored much more closely. And in the name of encouraging deep thinking and questioning of *all* sources of information, Michael often plays a game of telling "little white lies" to encourage his boys to pay attention to what people are really saying, and to speak up to adults when they detect deception. He also does it to get the boys to question things for themselves, to allow their creativity to flourish beyond what is commonly accepted as true. As a professional digital creator, Michael knows that exploring and building a possible truth requires a certain level of understanding and consistency to make it believable, and that sometimes to build new things you have to explore what does not yet exist.

With the challenges being faced globally today, and the ability of media to inform as well as deeply indoctrinate and influence our opinions and view of the world, how will you as a parent choose to address technology moving forward? Will you allow your child to independently consume the latest music and videos? Will you implement a technology diet and make discussing world events a top priority? Will encouraging deep thinking and questioning the sources and purposes of digital information make its way into your family routines? And, most importantly, will you take up the role in your family as the *technology leader* guiding your child's experiences in ways that are developmentally appropriate for his age and his ability to understand and digest the potent messages being shared globally?

Once you've considered how to approach technology philosophically, you'll need to grapple with the tools you'll choose. What sort of technologies will your child use to learn?

While tablets and smart phones are great for consuming digital content, they aren't the best tools for *creating* content. If you are considering an online cyber school, ask the staff if a computer is included with enrollment (it often is). If your child winds up in a cyber class, he or she will access an online classroom, often housed in what's called a "learning management system" (LMS). While tablets are fine for reading content in an LMS, they are less useful when it comes to posting thoughts and assignments online. Typing on a tablet screen can be done, but learning to touch type on a keyboard is not only more efficient, but a great lifelong skill that will serve your child well beyond his school career. You may also want to consider additional tools to serve your child's particular areas of interest. Many of today's kids are interested in creating videos, so you may consider the purchase of a decent digital camera and tripod. If your child is a maker or tinkerer, you might consider a 3D printer, as they have come down in price tremendously. Adding on some peripheral technologies to make learning more fun is a great way to keep your child interested and motivated all day long. As you continue to plan ahead, consider where your child will gather information and content, what your child will use as source material. If you're going with a cyber school option, you've likely seen the content she'll be learning from. Those resources may include paper-based textbooks as well as digital ones. The courses your child will take may also include instructors who can help build your child's skills in the area of determining reputable and authentic resources online. If you choose to go the independent or unschooling route, teaching online skills will become part of your repertoire. It's an awesome responsibility and task to think about how your child may grow to see the entire Internet as one of his main learning resources. By most accounts, today's kids use two main resources when they want to learn something new. Can you guess which two? Yup, Google and YouTube!

One of the great things about directing your child's learning is the chance you gain to really monitor and guide where the information she engages with comes from. As your child begins to explore areas of interest, either through projects in cyber school or through homeschooling options, he will likely need to make trips to the library for books or to conduct research online. Reviewing your child's plans and the information he's gathering is a great way to get to know your child and to encourage growth in new and exciting ways. In those conversations, you can touch on big ideas often overlooked in school such as:

- Where does knowledge come from?
- How do we know an idea is really true or not?
- What counts as a reliable source?

- How can I begin to trust my own instincts about what I'm reading?
- How can I share my thoughts with others who have different opinions or ideas on the topic?

Instead of your child answering the question, "What did you learn today?" with a blank stare or a simple, "Nothing," you'll now know what his mind has been up to, and what has captured his imagination.

Let's face it, we live in strange times. Having come through a presidential election that was unlike anything most of us have experienced before, many children are confused, scared, and shutting down. Teachers everywhere are continuing to focus on lessons about anti-bullying, interconnectedness, and basic human rights and dignity, while many adults on the planet – including in the highest of elected offices – display behaviors that directly oppose the ideals being taught. TV and social media, left unmonitored, are providing our youngsters with a steady barrage of stories about deception, starvation, war, death, and destruction.

Today's child, when plugged in, is being pumped with a steady diet of pain. Today's child is experiencing a level of fear not all that different from the description shared in this book's forward by PHM Atwater of her experiences as a child growing up during World War II. And without caring adults to talk with, today's child begins to numb out, shut down, or worse. More and more children are taking their own lives in order to avoid the pain they see day in and day out in the world around them.

The term "cognitive dissonance" is used in psychology to describe the emotional state we experience when our core beliefs and ideologies do not match our lived experience – when our inner and outer worlds are in conflict with each other. Cognitive dissonance is the lived experience of many children and adults alike in our world today – and it is creating dangerous levels of stress, anxiety, and anger. So what is a caring parent to do?

We've talked throughout this book about the importance of knowing your child and what motivates and excites her as well as what challenges and terrifies her. We've talked about how to identify or create a safe haven for learning. The conversations you've had may have also included your child's feelings about big global issues and challenges. It will be important for you to continue to talk with your child about the world we now are living in and how the dissonance is impacting his thinking, his hopes and dreams, his heart. Encouraging philosophical dialogue, gently guiding your child to understand contradiction and irony using the mechanisms of curiosity and logic can provide a relief valve. Where many believe that such dialogue is not appropriate until high school, I believe we must begin to have these sorts of conversations as soon as our children begin to wonder, begin to question, begin to feel afraid to wake up in the morning.

As caring adults it's our moral duty, as PMH Atwater described from her own experiences, to see the little child sobbing at the sight of so many gold stars, to listen to the terror of her knowing that cherished adults have passed, to her wondering about her own life and death and the meaning of it all. It is our sacred duty to take that terrified child into our arms, to make things as safe as we can, but more importantly to hold space for fear and worry to be released, and cultivating hope and joy for the future as often as possible.

I believe that you wouldn't be here reading this book if you weren't ready or up to this monumental task. Bravo!

Many of today's spiritual teachers believe that we each possess an innate and often untapped genius that can be activated through investigating things that interest us. Our brilliance is shared with the world through creating masterpieces that demonstrate our creative ideas. They also believe that everything there is to know is accessible to each and every one of us. Some of the methods proposed are ones you and your child are likely to experience as you organize yourselves for learning in more open and creative ways. By following the interests of your child, you will notice big changes in confidence as well as interest in learning. Kids who are given the chance to explore what they love are generally happier, more focused, and more successful in their learning. They are able to tap into their personal genius!

Now that you've gotten things prepared for your child, the last big item on your to do list for this chapter is to consider yourself. Yup. It's time to think about you, and your own inner child.

Making a change to either cyber learning or homeschooling likely means that your child will be around the house more often, which may impact your own personal or business plans in interesting ways. Whether you have a work-from-home business or will be supporting your child's learning, you will be modeling work and play habits for your child. For instance, if your child plans to study during the hours of 10 am to 2 pm, you may want to complete the bulk of your personal or business work during that same timeframe. You and your child can schedule lunch together some days, or you can encourage your child to take care of his own noon time meal, depending on his age and maturity. Using an organizer or the weekly planning document from my website will help you prepare for your own week so that it aligns in ways that encourage and support your child.

Be sure to consider the togetherness factor. That is, how will you handle being around your child 24/7 every day of the year? Will you need to schedule time apart? Will you need to come up with strategies to handle disagreements? It's impractical to think you will be able to live, sleep, and learn/work together without some occasional disagreements or challenges occurring. How will you get the time you need for yourself? How will you communicate when it's okay for your child to interrupt your work? How will you build strength and resiliency in your child so that he tries tackling issues on his own in several ways before coming to you for help? We'll touch on some tips and tricks for building an independent learner in our next chapter.

Chapter 9

Getting Going!

"To sentence a man of true genius to the drudgery of a school
is to put a racehorse on a treadmill."
- Samuel Taylor Coleridge

Welcome to day one of this new learning adventure with your child! By this time you've likely done one of three things: you've asked for changes to be made in your child's learning situation at his current school, you've changed schools, or you've chosen to have your child learn from home. Now we'll tackle some of the steps you can take to get going.

If you've chosen to work with your child's teacher on making school better, there are a few additional tips I can offer. In my current professional life as an educational consultant, I offer masters-level courses to teachers who are currently working in a classroom. The work focuses on student-centered, inquiry-based learning. In the online courses, we use inquiry methods in order to learn more about educational concepts and how to apply them in the classroom. In a nutshell, inquiry-based learning begins with a question and proceeds forward with an individualized investigation of the ideas and to test concepts, ultimately arriving at some personal conclusions. Inquiry is the way in which many kids truly flourish as learners, and it's a method you can use with your child.

In one of the classes, we investigate mindful practices for a teacher's personal benefit as well as for inclusion in the classroom. My students try on breathing activities, yoga, and mindful awareness activities for themselves, while reflecting in class upon their impact. Throughout the course, our focus is on becoming aware of our thinking, creating space between thoughts and habitual reactions, and choosing to respond from a place of clarity. These techniques are useful for all children, and especially for those who are part of traditional education settings. If school is beginning to work for your child, adding in mindful practices can serve him well as he continues to grow and thrive in school.

A search on the terms "mindfulness for kids" will help you to locate websites, organizations, videos, and activities to try out together in order to develop the ability to bring attention away from negative thinking and to a more peaceful calm place. It's from that quiet space that your child can then find freedom both in and out of school. *Mindful Child* and *Mindful Games*, both by author Susan Kaiser Greenland, are two great reads to support mindful practice with kids. Both books focus on activities that will help your child become calmer, more focused, and happier, both inside and outside of the classroom.

If you've chosen to change schools, you'll be starting over fresh with a new blank slate, so to speak. What a wonderful opportunity for you and your child to create the kind of learning experience that you've been dreaming of! Now is the time to take a look at what kind of inner work might be needed in order to create that ideal outcome. Our inside landscape has a lot to do with the outside circumstances in our lives.

Many of today's wisdom teachers talk about looking at circumstances as the outside manifestation of our inner processes. They also urge us to understand that things are as they are, and then we add thoughts. Our thoughts about the circumstances begin to color in the story to suit our beliefs and agreements about how life should be. In becoming aware of this process, we then become able to stand as a neutral witness to our thinking. This allows us the freedom to choose how to see things differently in any moment, versus being trapped in our habitual thought patterns.

I'd like you to think back to the exercises you and your child completed in order to consider what learning situation suited them. At that time, your child had stated in some manner that they hated school. By asking some simple questions and digging deeper into the story, did you determine that the issues ran deeper than just curriculum, boredom, bullying, or conflicts with the teacher or classmates? You likely noticed that your child was seeking your attention with his statements and behavior. Perhaps you recognized that the statement was expressing a request for your help, a need to live and learn in a way more aligned with who he is and hopes to be.

If you've chosen to homeschool or use a cyber school provider, you are in for a grand adventure. Having your child at home while you supervise their learning or do your own home-based business work is an amazing opportunity for you both to grow and learn. The added togetherness will surely push boundaries for everyone, which is a great way to learn more about your child. Sure, there will be days when you and your kid want to kill each other. That's when having other homeschool families, colleagues, or friends to rely upon will help tremendously.

This is the point where it is useful for us to figure out precisely what it is you will do to screw things up – and to figure out solutions to the problems before they arise. When we do anything new, there's often a small part of ourselves that is afraid to step into the unknown, to be bold, to do things differently than they've been done before. It's the part of us that feels safer in what's known vs. what's unknown. As poet Hama Tuma put it, we are "happier with the devil we know than the angel we don't know." I love the positive spin on the old phrase, showing us that often the thing we fear the most is actually a really good outcome!

I've included an appendix that lists the most common fears and FAQs parents have while making an educational change on behalf of their child. It's useful to review them as they'll help you identify some of the sabotage mechanisms that are likely to crop up. They include worries about what others will think about your plans, the reasons you're too busy to make this work, and so on. Recognize that all of these fears are actually excuses for not making your child's life more bearable and actually enjoyable.

It's also possible that your own inner child is the culprit. So often, because we didn't get to have the childhood we wanted, because we were forced to go to schools that didn't fit, we agree with the notion that school is mandatory and the only course of action. As we've discovered, while there are laws that require your child to attend, there are workarounds that can be more freeing for you and your child. In a nutshell, don't let your fears keep you from healing your child and your own inner child. Choose a more joyful educational experience.

In my own life, it's taken nearly 50 years to realize that I am capable of following my passions and my heart, creating the life I always dreamed of. It took living through and becoming part of the big system of school as a student, then teacher and administrator, to recognize that there isn't one best way to do anything, and that school isn't the only way to learn. It took losing a job and deciding to forge my own pathways for me to see that I was responsible for making my own life. Taking responsibility for my own life has helped me learn to nurture things that bring me joy, ease and freedom. After realizing I could do things differently, I decided to share that wisdom with teachers, encouraging them to use inquiry, mindfulness, and technology to release children to their own curiosities and passions to motivate growth as learners.

And you're part of my story too! Regardless of the choices you make, it's all working out perfectly – especially when you can see the world and your life as one enormous classroom, with everyone and everything serving as your teachers. I'm here to support and guide you as you make changes.

If you think about what we've learned about the system of school, you'll see that it primarily operates to dispense content in a prescribed manner in a particular timeframe. Covering prescribed curriculum dominates the day. Rigid curriculum leads to standardized vs. individualized learning. Whether we realize it or not, it sends the subliminal message that there is one right way to do things. It assumes that one way of doing also works for everyone. And you are part of a growing number of families who have decided to make a change!

You and I recognize that compulsory education is not for everyone. We see that school doesn't have to feel like prison. We know that learning is an organic process, especially when it's open and provides a learner with the freedom to be himself.

We also know that emotions and feelings aren't a bad thing. We recognize that they point to things that aren't working for kids, and we know how to use the information to determine new ways of thinking and seeing the world. We can see that learning that is open, self-determined, and self-organized allows children to learn "how to think" vs. "what to think." It's a wonderful difference, and with just a bit of effort, it can be life-changing. You and your child are well on the way to making this your new reality!

So how will you know that you've reached your goal of helping your child love learning again? Perhaps your success will look something like the outcome my friends Becky and Rose have seen. In Rose's case, homeschool felt like a better fit than a traditional high school after having attended a small Catholic school for elementary and middle school. Where Rose struggled to adapt to the big classes, a feeling of being invisible, and the slow pace of the curriculum, she is now thriving doing online curriculum and creating her own learning pathways with the help of her mom. She spends time in the local coffee shop not only getting her school work done, but learning more about life from the caring adults who come in and out of the store for business meetings. And she has developed friendships with caring members of the community. Whereas once everyone in the family questioned Becky's sanity in pulling Rose out of school, and worried about her socialization, they now see Rose thriving and growing into young adulthood as a self-actualized individual.

Your success might just as well look like Kim and Kileigh's. Ki is thriving at his local middle school, while collaborating with a team of adults on holidays, evenings, and weekends to build a new micro-school for kids in the area. He treats his time in the traditional school setting as an investigator or a detective might. He has an intense curiosity to learn about what it's like to be in a big public school after having attended a small progressive school for three years. Ki is documenting what works, what doesn't, and sharing what he thinks all kids need to be successful in life with the school-building team. He's providing critical information to the team about what life is like for today's teens, helping the team dream up innovative solutions.

I'd like to offer some tips for the road as you begin your journey together in the coming weeks and months:

- Day 1 – take time to notice this first day. Take some pictures, keep a journal. This learning journey is brand new and worth documenting. Make time to celebrate your decision to choose something different.

- Week 1 – notice how the week went. What worked? What didn't? Take time to talk about the changes you can make to continue to make the learning setting even better. If your child is still in a school setting, call or email the teacher to follow up on what's changed for the positive. If you're trying cyber school or an unschooling option, talk about your experiences with family and friends. Help them to see the ways in which your choices are helping your child develop a love of learning. Most importantly, share the benefits you've seen in communicating more clearly with your child about school and learning.

- Month 1 – take time to look back on the past four weeks. Have things improved at school? Have things not improved? Take time to meet with your child's teacher again to discuss what you've noticed and to make adjustments to the plan or to move forward with a teacher or school change. If things are working and your child's attitude toward school is improving, the teacher will surely enjoy the positive feedback. Perhaps you can come up with even more ideas about how to keep your child engaged and content in the classroom! If you've chosen cyber or homeschooling, this is a great time to begin planning ahead. What will you do differently in the coming month?

- Year 1 – as you come up on a year, consider revisiting the exercises outlined in this book again. Compare your child's responses to feelings about school and learning from when you started with her responses today. Ask questions about what she is really interested in pursuing going forward. And make adjustments to your plans or modify the processes you've put in place where needed.

You can make changes for your child at any point during the journey. You don't have to wait until the end of a year. Sure, there are timelines to follow related to applications for charter or private schools, and if you think that's something you'd like to offer your child at some point, you'll want to keep those in mind as you go along. Otherwise, know that you can make changes to cyber school or homeschool any time of the year. Families who have to change schools because of work or moving do it with success all the time, therefore so can you. You'll want to be cautious about overdoing it. With any changes, it makes sense to take some time to really test out the new setting and to try and determine why it's not working before making changes again.

I'd love to hear about how it's going for you and your child. Best of luck on the journey!

Conclusion

*"You cannot teach a man anything; you can only help him to
find it within himself."*

- Galileo Galilei

E arlier in the book, I mentioned the notion of *child whispering*. You
can now count yourself as a person who is developing this very
same set of skills. You've practiced recognizing and advocating
for the situations and activities that make your child sparkle. You've
learned to listen to your child deeply, and to hear the words behind the
complaints or refusals to go to school as a plea for change.

Perhaps you've uncovered some old pain around your own experiences
related to school. Perhaps your parents were unable to see and hear you
clearly and offer you an appropriate change. If so, I recommend taking
time to grieve that truth and to understand that your parents did the best
they could for you based on what they'd experienced. You've learned so
much and grown beyond that limited reality – otherwise you wouldn't
be here reading this book. Just the fact that you're willing to see and hear
your child is a remarkable feat, and I for one am very proud of you!

This book hasn't been so much about making your kid love the school he has been attending as it has been all about discovering why your child hates it so much. It's been about learning to love that strength in your kid, the anger that fueled his voice to speak personal truth. It's been about seeing who your child is, deep down, and being ok with him as he is. Your child is an adult in the making and she just wants it to be ok to be herself, to have fun, to feel free, to be loved, and most importantly to be accepted just as she is. You've worked through the steps in this book and you've come a long way toward helping her become that amazing person she dreams of becoming.

This book has actually been more about you than your child. It's been about making a decision, even if it's been difficult, to make changes to help your child grow and thrive. It's been about stepping up to the plate and taking charge of your child's education, even if no one made those kinds of choices for you as a child.

It has also subtly been about forgiving *your* teachers, *your* parents, and even yourself for not always being present in the ways that helped you feel whole. By being there for your child, you have been subtly healing your own inner child. This book has been about coming to a place of peace and acceptance around school and your past experiences with it. It has been about recognizing that all of the adults in your life were doing the best they could with the information they had at the time, just as you have with your child. Perhaps you've begun to see your own challenges with school as a catalyst. They prepared you to be ready, willing, and able to make things even better for your own child.

Our stories have a lot in common. We went to school, we tried our best, we conformed when we could, rebelled when we had to, and we made it through somehow. We grew up believing that everyone should go to school, even though that didn't always feel quite right in our tummies. And now we know enough that we want something different for our kids than to just require them to repeat the pattern of school, because someone out there says they have to, or just because we had to. We know that there are real options for freedom that can be put in place with just a bit of effort. We know that it's possible to create whatever we want when we put our mind to it first – tacking the old gremlins as they come up, making friends with the "enemy" of fear, knowing that fear points the quickest way to freedom.

I was talking with Dean in his mom's rock shop one day. I told him about my dream of creating a small school for kids who were tapped in to their passions, who knew what they wanted to do in the world to help make it a better place. I still remember his response like it was yesterday. He looked deeply into my eyes and said, "Mara, I want you to build that school here for me." It's been a few years since that conversation, but not a day has gone by that I haven't thought about him or worked on some idea or other related to building that type of school for Dean and other kids like him. And I can report that the dream is closer to a reality today than it was back then.

My reason for sharing the small school story is two-fold. I hope you'll recognize that you've grown in your ability to see and hear a child in the same manner that I do with Dean. I also hope you'll recognize the power that comes from truly being in service to a child who has passion for living. I believe that I'm here on this planet at this precise moment in time to help offer new and different learning options for kids. I coach parents and kids nearly every day in taking back their personal power and responsibility for learning – and it's a job I truly love! I revel in watching the incredible transformation that occurs when my clients begin to tap into their own purpose and passion by beginning to following their own independent learning pathways. I love to hear about the new ideas they are exploring and the connections between ideas they've found, ones that only they can see because of the unique way in which they experience the world.

Nearly every day, as a consultant, mentor and coach, I get to have a WIFL day. One of my friends coined the acronym to capture the words "What I Feel Like." In working for myself as a learner first, I follow the path of least resistance, doing the things I love. This is what I wish for you and your child. That learning becomes second nature, like breathing, and that it becomes a joyful act which feeds personal inquiry and growth for a lifetime.

Remember the movie *Avatar* and the way in which the Na'vi on Pandora greeted one another with the words, "I see you"? That sentiment has a very similar feel to the Hindi greeting, namaste, which means, "the light in me sees the light in you." This process of addressing your child's apparent hatred of school has been a profound act of love on your part. It has allowed you to see and hear your child in new ways. By working together to create a new plan of action around school, you've joined together as learning teammates. And a grand adventure lies ahead for you both.

One of my favorite authors is an African elder and teacher, Malidoma Patrice Some. Dr. Some is a shaman from the Dagara tribe in Burkina Faso. In describing his culture's beliefs surrounding children, he shares an incredible ritual where elders communicate with each unborn child in order to determine its purpose for reincarnating and the gifts it will be bringing to benefit the tribe. After birth, the child is named related to his or her intended purpose. During the birth ritual, every member of the community celebrates the child with a commitment to supporting a successful life.

Can you imagine this sort of ritual and ceremony in our current culture? How would things be different if you had been told why your child had chosen you as a parent and what she was coming into the world to accomplish? Would it have changed how you've done things to help him along the way? In a way, the steps outlined in this book are my attempt to create new rituals that address the deep potential of your child, now that she is here on the planet. Even if we never have the same level of awareness the Dargara have, you and I have taken a step forward toward creating a culture where caring adults put the learning needs of their children at the top of the priority list. We're making sure that your child isn't left behind, rather than relying on the educational legislation with a similar name.

In some places on our planet, in Bhutan for example, the measure of success in life isn't related to "gross domestic product," but rather "gross domestic happiness." The work you've done to help your child find joy in learning is a pointer in that same direction. Sure, being content while learning often leads to tremendous creativity, and wealth is sometimes the byproduct. But you've put your child's happiness first, which is a tremendous achievement.

If, for any reason, you begin to doubt yourself along the way, just check out the stories of presidents Washington, Lincoln, Truman, Cleveland, Taylor, or Johnson. Their educational preparations were not nearly as robust as yours and mine, and yet they became the top leaders of our nation. *The belief we've long shared, that education = success, can no longer be taken as an absolute truth.* School works for many, and does not, for many more. You've now joined the proud ranks of those who are willing to try something different in order to offer your child the best future possible.

Parting Thoughts

As a parent, grandparent, caregiver, or loved one, what is your wildest dream come true for that special child in your life? If you've made it this far, then I imagine your dream statement might read something like this:

"Since we created a change in the way our son is educated, he is happier, much more healthy, and flourishing!"

or

"My foster daughter now loves to learn and is curious about everything around her!"

or

"My grandson begs to go to the library for books, longs to create things with his hands, and is bright and cheerful with everyone he meets."

or

"My step-daughter is now motivated by an inner drive, a mission. She knows what she wants to do with her life and is well on her way to making it a reality!"

or perhaps

"My son has published his first book and is following in my footsteps. He's building his own business based on the things he loves most in the world. I'm thrilled to be sharing this adventure with him!"

Are you excited by the statements above? Do you feel like this is where you want your child to be? Do you have absolutely no idea how to make it happen? Do you feel fear when you think about making any kind of changes to your child's education? If you answered yes to any of these questions, you are in the right place at the right time. You are on the threshold of something new, something awesome. You can totally do this!

We are going to wrap up our adventure here together in a bit of an unconventional way. You've obviously made a commitment to change the educational opportunities and outcomes for your child. To ensure that becomes a reality for you, let's visualize your success together. By envisioning the place you intend to be, you will clarify your goals, making it much easier to follow the path toward them. Creating a big, bold, audacious picture of the future, you will set yourself up for amazing success!

We both know that your child has been suffering in some way, related to experiences at school. Let's put down those images for a moment. You know them all too well, because you've worried about your child multiple times a day for years. In the past chapters, you've made lists of what's not working, you have some idea what your child wants related to school. You know that they need something different. But by continuing to focus on the image of your child in pain, we are inadvertently creating barriers to quickly changing the situation. By focusing on what you don't want, you actually create more of it. So let's drop the apparent reality of the situation for a moment and imagine that things could be different for your child. Much better! So, what is it you imagine for your child?

Take a moment, clear your mind. A few deep belly breaths will help. Inhale through your nose and exhale through your mouth, slowly and deeply. Close your eyes and let go of any negative feelings or emotions you may be sensing at the moment. Relax your body, working your way up from the feet to the crown of your head. Notice where your body is feeling tension and imagine the muscles as a rubber band being pulled too tight. Now imagine the tension letting go and exhale. Continue to breathe in and out until you feel relaxed and light.

Now imagine your child at their very best. Happy. Healthy. Engaged. Creative. Content. Full of curiosity. Picture your child bubbling with enthusiasm, rushing into your arms and talking a mile a minute, bursting with the new ideas that they've just learned!

Hold that image in your mind. Revel in the lightness of the feeling, the joyfulness of the emotions, and the peace and bliss that are pouring from your child. Take a picture of that child in your mind's eye at this very moment. Turn it into a hologram, capturing the image from every angle. Now imagine a place to store this memory, perhaps in a treasure chest, for safekeeping.

Come back to this image over and over as you work through the school changes you've chosen to make for your child. This is the image of your child in the not-too-distant future. And with each word you re-

read, each activity you complete together, and each action you take to move your child's educational experience forward, you will be one step closer to meeting that child in the flesh. Congratulations on taking this first bold step toward making it happen, for yourself and your child!

To enhance this meditation experience, you both might enjoy making a vision board. Take a poster board or bulletin board and cover it with pictures, magazine clippings, words, and phrases that resemble the future you want for your child, the desired outcome. You might include pictures of happy, healthy engaged kids. Your vision board might include pictures of new kinds of classrooms, the woods, the library, or any other sorts of activities you'd like to see your child engaged in more often.

Creating the vision board will help you to maintain a positive focus when your resolve wavers. It will help you and your child stay focused on figuring out the very best educational setting for success and happiness. Knowing what it looks like, feels like, smells like, ahead of time increases the chances of its manifestation and ensures your success.

If I can be of service to you and your family, now or in the future, you are welcome to contact me via email at: mlinaberger@gmail.com. I look forward to hearing your stories, learning about your successes, and supporting you in your adventure, should you need some help along the way!

Appendix: FEARS & FAQs

*"Between stimulus and response there is a space. In that space is
our power to choose our response. In our response lies our growth
and our freedom."*
- **Viktor Frankl**, *Man's Search for Meaning*

Fear. Such a loaded word. I'm guessing you've felt it bubble up inside you at least once while you've been reading this book. It seems that most of the challenges parents report when addressing issues or making choices to change their child's education come from a place of fear. So next we'll bring all those to light. Have you ever heard the acronym for fear: *False Evidence Appearing Real?* Pretty powerful. True fear is a biological response, something that alerts us to life-threatening situations and helps us to respond quickly and efficiently. In the case of tending to your child's issues around school, most often the issues are not life or death. Though if they are, all the more reason to create your plan and get moving.

When fear is based on false evidence it is a decoy; it's an internal avoidance mechanism we each use to derail our best efforts. Such fears can only exist when you fuel them. One of the most efficient ways to disempower your fears is by naming them and then looking at the truth of what can actually be done. It's like creating an antidote! To ensure your success, let's name some common fears you may have and identify their antidotes.

FEAR: If I take my child out of school, my neighbor (ex, friend, enemy, _____) might call social services and report me as being an unfit parent.

Antidote: The best antidote to this fear is planning, preparation, and documentation. If you've gone through the previous chapters and have worked with your child step by step to determine the best fit for him or her educationally, you'll have little or nothing to fear. Create an established routine – stick to it – and keep documentation. You can also join a homeschool association, which often provides legal counsel on such matters should anyone choose to challenge the choices you've made to benefit your child's specific learning needs. If social services does appear, you'll be able to joyfully share all the amazing progress your child has made as a cyber or homeschooler.

FEAR: I'm not qualified, don't have enough education or credentials, or am not smart enough to support my child's learning.

Antidote: By definition, as long as you know more than your child, you are qualified to teach her something you know. And most communities now have a homeschool co-op where you can collaborate with others to offer your child access to knowledge or experiences that you don't possess. You can also lean on the wisdom of museums, galleries, and online curriculum to bolster what you don't know. Best of all, why not turn learning into a fun inquiry activity for you both – learning, side by side, the topics your child finds of interest?

FEAR: My child won't have friends, won't be socialized, and will grow up to be a recluse or deviant or worse.

Antidote: This fear couldn't be farther from the truth. If you choose to cyber or homeschool your child, they will have access to you, your family, other siblings, and neighborhood friends. And assuming that you have attracted amazing folks around you, your child will be learning from the very best! If you belong to a church or co-op, your child will gain wisdom from those peers as well. Honestly, just take a look at the culture of school today reported in the news. With so much focus on competition, testing, and the like, not to mention the proliferation of drugs, alcohol and sex, do you really think that school can guarantee your child a superior socialization than the one you can provide?

FEAR: My child won't get into college, or he'll be a failure at adult life if he doesn't get a traditional high school diploma.

Antidote: As the number of homeschoolers rises, so do the number of students who are accepted by traditional colleges. In fact, an increasing number of colleges are actively recruiting students who have been homeschooled, finding them to be far more creative and independent as learners. In most cases, homeschoolers who want to attend college are asked to show evidence of learning through portfolios, transcripts created by their parents, or by providing scores from either the SAT or ACT exams. As the trend in homeschooling continues, so will the ability for these students to apply to the colleges of their choice. Sitting for the GED exam is always an option for your child – in fact, many homeschoolers pass the exam well ahead of their schooled counterparts, and enter college early as well.

FEAR: My family, spouse, or close friends will judge me, say I'm crazy, make me feel bad about my choices, or even turn their backs on me.

Antidote: This is one of those cases where you are going to have to dig deep inside yourself. There is plenty of evidence out there that homeschooling is neither freakish nor harmful to children. Having worked yourself through this book and the exercises, you are well-informed and have the ability to stand up to naysayers with gentle confidence. Not only that, you clearly know what would make your child happy and what would benefit her educationally. Tackling this fear is about learning to stand up for yourself and your child. It's not about doing what's popular or traditional, but about doing what's best for your child. If spouses, friends, or family can't support that, are they really worth worrying about?

FEAR: My kid will end up hating me if I make him do his work at home.

Antidote: This is highly unlikely at this point if you've been talking with your child all along. It's also unlikely that you are going to assign lots of homework to your child. Once the learning day is done, he or she should be free to explore independent topics. In fact, it's more probable that your child will end up liking you more if you choose to make educational choices on his behalf.

Now that we've tackled the big fears many parents have, you may have some lingering questions. Left unaddressed, they can also serve as obstacles and avoidance mechanisms, which can potentially derail your plans in moving forward.

QUESTION: What should we do if we don't have the money to pay for the private, alternative or cyber we've chosen for our child?

Solution: Many private schools and alternatives offer partial scholarships for students in need. In some cases, parents can offer to do work in exchange for a reduction in tuition. In the case of cyber schools, if one is operating as a charter in your state, tuition will likely cost you nothing. Don't let money get in the way of your child's learning. Ask questions, ask for help, and take action to make it work for your child.

QUESTION: What if I'm not able (or neither of us, in a two-parent household, is able) to be at home all day to support my child in cyber or homeschool?

Solution: In regards to an adult being at home to supervise homeschooling, there are several options. Check in with your local homeschooling group to see if other parents might agree to collaborate with you in leading learning days for kids. Basically each of you covers a day or two a week, allowing you to address your individual work schedules in creative ways. Perhaps you'll also consider this as an opportunity to start that home-based business you've always dreamed of. If your bank account is flush, there is also the option of hiring a professional tutor, or securing a tutor with a couple of friends. In most states, a tutor can work with up to four children without having to set up legally as a school. There are plenty of options out there. Do some searching. Ask some questions. Get creative!

QUESTION: How do we address the more creative subjects like art, music, dance, theater, and sports?

Solution: This is where alternative education excels! The creative arts and sports are one of the reasons many parents choose to homeschool or cyber school their kids. Completing traditional content in a more efficient manner will create more time in the day to take private lessons in the arts, or to spend time in sports instruction or activities. Many parents don't realize that their child may still be eligible to participate in his home school district's sports programs. Check with a district administrator to learn more about the options available for your child.

QUESTION: What do we do about achievement testing, SATs/ACTs, and college selection, application, enrollment, scholarships, and student loans?

Solution: If you homeschool your child, you may be asked to participate in state-mandated testing by your local district, and many private schools and alternatives administer some sort of achievement testing with students as well. In most cases achievement testing is optional. If you'd like your child to skip the testing for emotional or religious reasons, you are legally allowed to opt out. As for taking SATs and ACTs for college entrance, those will be up to you to schedule, should your child's college of choice require them as part of her applications package. Most local libraries have someone on staff who is familiar with the college applications, student loans, and scholarships and can support many of the same functions a high school guidance counselor does.

QUESTION: I actually run a home-based business and don't think I can monitor my child's learning every day. What should I do?

Solution: This is a tough call. You might follow the same steps as the parents who need options that align with work outside the home (such as working with a co-op or hiring a tutor to outsource the tasks). Ask yourself, however, how much time it would take to train your child to work independently by your side? And what would be the ultimate benefit to your kid doing his school work while you tend to your business? What lessons might you both gain? I encourage you to consider trading some of your business focus up front in order to help your child become an independent learner by your side. He'll learn far more from watching your business interactions than you think. He might even end up being one of your employees or your business partner some day!

QUESTION: What if I don't want to (or don't know how to) deal with all the paperwork?

Solution: Most of the paperwork required in changing schools is a one-shot deal. Just take it step by step, and ask for help from school staff where you need it. Depending on your choices for homeschooling and the age of your child, the paperwork doesn't have to be the nightmare that most parents think it will be. Once your child has been properly signed out of school and you've determined the evidence you'll need to collect, your child can actually take the lead on creating the homeschool binder for submission. If your child is tech-savvy, he or she can actually create a digital portfolio using online tools as part of a daily or weekly routine. If you go the cyber route, most of the paperwork will be taken care of for you. If you just don't have time or the energy to deal with it, you can contract with an educational consultant (such as myself) to complete the paperwork and/or documentation.

As we wrap up this section, I'd like to tell you about my friend Pam. She called one afternoon last fall to talk about her daughter's ongoing issues in school. Pam's husband had recently died after a long and difficult battle with a degenerative disease, and the struggles, emotionally, spiritually, and physically, had taken their toll on everyone.

Pam's daughter Melissa had been refusing to go to school for some time, chalking up her disinterest to her troubles with "mean girls" in class. The family had started counseling and Melissa was getting the best support possible for working slowly through grief and anger around her dad's death. Pam and Melissa had also already worked through the first few layers of the processes I've outlined in the previous chapters – and they'd determined that the best course of action was to move Melissa to the local Catholic school. When Pam called, Melissa was dealing with truancy issues again and things had escalated to the point where Pam was going to have to consider moving her daughter to yet another school if things didn't improve.

I went out for dinner with Pam, Melissa, and Melissa's younger brother for dinner one evening to get a sense of what the core issues might be. While we were having dinner, Melissa was on her cell phone texting with friends and posting pictures of our meal to Snapchat. Pam had gotten Melissa the latest iPhone shortly after her husband's death as a distraction, as something to help ease the pain. I wondered about whether or not the gift was helping Melissa's grief or actually creating more pain.

We talked a little more after dinner about Melissa's core issues in school. Pam shared that Melissa often used her phone to text back and forth with other girls in her classes and that sometimes the texts escalated into name-calling and bullying. She had looked at some of the texts and had recognized that often it was Melissa's hasty responses and misinterpretations of other girls' messaging that were ultimately creating the biggest problems. We chatted about the family counseling they were receiving and about Melissa's continued resistance to going to school. One of Pam's and my shared "ah-ha moments" came when we recognized that no matter where Melissa chose to go to school she would need to do some deep work related to her dad's death and her own feelings of inadequacy. We realized that no matter where she went, her problems would follow, as they were not specifically related to school itself, but rather to grief, self-love, and to her lack of clear communication skills. I think Pam and Melissa's story points to the core of what we've been working toward throughout this entire book, whether you've realized it or not. We've been working around the notion of our thoughts creating our experience of life. When we feel happy and content, everything appears bright and joyous. When we feel sadness and dissolution, that's the reflection we see in our outside world. In Melissa's sadness and anger over her father's death, she was seeing rejection and abandonment in her friends, when what she needed most was love and acceptance, and time to heal amongst trusted confidants.

You've spent a lot of time with your child, talking about school, what works and what doesn't. You know what the core issues are. You've been building a stronger relationship with your child through the communications about school and the planning activities. Most important to remember moving forward is to keep those clear lines of communication open, and focus more on what's working than on what isn't. You've been creating the kind of stable foundation your child needs to rebuild her self-esteem as a learner.

In truth, the externals, the particulars of what you end up choosing for your child school-wise, are far less important than the new, budding relationship you've been building. Clear communication, unwavering support, and most of all unconditional love – those are the real things your child was saying he needed back when he first told you he hated school. You've come a long way since that day and you've likely begun to see how little it really had to do with school at all.

Afterword

You've just had a penetrating and practical conversation with a veteran insider, a gifted teacher who was fortunate enough to work in a "good" school. It was one where autonomy, flexibility, and originality had not yet been wiped out by the current plague of federal mandates and also where the principal really was everyone's pal. He encouraged the teachers to care and to inject their personal talents into their work. Even so, under conditions a vast majority of educators would deem practically utopian, Mara became more and more disheartened by the realization that the large size of her class and the ever more relentless demands of the curriculum were making it impossible to meet the individual needs, and nurture the individual gifts, of far too many of her students. When she fully awakened to the reality that she was no longer able to serve as the facilitator, mentor, and source of inspiration she had felt called to be, and instead was forced to herd sheep and manage a factory floor, she knew it was time to move on.

Thankfully, that same calling has led Mara to turn what she learned during her 25 years in the classroom into a lifeline for young people stuck in schools that do not suit them. Indeed, as Mara warns, when children say they hate school they're sending out a distress signal. Something is dreadfully wrong, and everyone who plays an important role in their lives should listen immediately and not dismiss it as just another childhood complaint like hating broccoli or having snarled hair brushed out. The response must not be, "Yeah, I hated school when I was a kid, too, but I made it thorough okay…. Don't worry, so will you." And don't for even a moment consider it might be your children's fault.

Mara is right. No one blames their feet when their shoes don't fit. They find a pair that does.

The fact of the matter is that every child is born with a unique developmental trajectory. No two kids learn in exactly the same way. Nor are any two developmentally primed to learn exactly the same things at exactly the same time either. Nature intends there to be as much of this kind of diversity as possible because, as evolution teaches us, the species with the most built-in diversity are the ones with the best chance to survive and thrive.

Therefore the idea of standardizing educational content and insisting that all children absorb it according to the same timetable is complete and utter nonsense. Based on the scathing things he once had to say about his own schooling, Einstein would without a doubt agree that a one-size-fits-all approach to education meets his definition of insanity to a "T." How can it possibly work when it so defies the laws of nature?

Children are also born with a highly accurate instinct to go after what they need right when they need it – unless of course their inner knowing has been beaten or sweetened out of them. Given the opportunity to do so, they will continually seek out exactly the right challenges that will spur their natural pursuit of knowledge and mastery. This is no longer just a philosophical belief; it is now scientific fact.

There is a rapidly growing body of research in biology, psychology, child development, cognitive science, and neuroscience showing that children truly come into the world with their own inner guidance. It is exquisitely calibrated to operate on a frequency that is theirs and theirs alone. They don't need to be nudged forward because they are inexorably driven to learn – even inside the womb! Their motivation comes from within, not from without. Moreover, countless studies now confirm that the kinds of external motivators upon which the factory school model so heavily depends actually interfere with deep learning and high performance.

We now know that the way children learn best is through self-directed exploration and discovery, not by others force-feeding them predigested bits of skills and information. Evolution has exquisitely adapted the brain for just this purpose by arranging it so that children automatically pursue what is interesting and meaningful to them. And they don't stop until each new investigation is complete.

But our schools continue to be informed by hundred-year-old theories that have turned out not to be true. And as Mara so rightly pointed out, nearly all of our schools remain stuck in a factory mode that may have been appropriate a century ago, but that is guaranteed to leave young people ill-prepared to deal with the fast-changing and uncertain world of today. What kids need now are schools where they develop the ability to think for themselves, and improvise, and work together to come up with creative solutions to complex problems.

So yes, all you newly awakened parents out there, if your children are telling you they hate school then it's time to take action. Trust that you and your children know what they need better than anyone else. Shake off any fear of questioning authority that you may have picked up when you were in school. Shed the urge to passively go along with the herd. But don't hesitate to follow Mara's amazing program for identifying exactly how your children's schools don't fit them and for creating a different situation that does. I know firsthand that Mara deeply knows of what she speaks because for the past six months she has been enrolled in the Alternative Education Resource Organization's School Starters

Program, of which I am a co-facilitator. We have been helping Mara and her team to crystallize their vision of a school kids will love going to everyday, and how to bring it into being. She truly is a "child whisperer," and she thoroughly understands the art of the possible.

If I may be so bold, in closing I would just like to add one more option to Mara's list of things to try. If, by chance, you happen to reach the end of it without finding the solution that works for you and your child, then consider creating an alternative of your own. Starting a school or a learning center is a challenging task to be sure, but it's actually how a great many of the current new wave of alternatives are born.

Best wishes to you.

Chris Mercogliano,
March 2017

Author of: ***In Defense of Childhood: Protecting Kids' Inner Wildness; How to Grow a School: Starting and Sustaining Schools That Work; Teaching the Restless: One School's Remarkable No-Ritalin Approach to Helping Children Learn and Succeed;*** and ***Making It Up As We Go Along: The Story of the Albany Free School***

Acknowledgements

My passion for learning was kindled as a child growing up in my maternal grandmother's house. It was my grandma Lois' encouragement of my musical talents, combined with my mom Elsa's dedication to my lessons and practice, and my dad Jim's financial and moral supports, that helped me build a lifelong passion for learning. The lessons I mastered around diligent practice, creating harmony, and the ability to listen to the spaces between the notes, have served me well.

To my family: my sisters Anne and Betsy, their husbands Tom and Brian, my nephews JT and Liam, my step-mother Sandi, and to my extended family of aunts, uncles, cousins, and step-siblings, I'm grateful for the love you've offered as I've charted my own way along the winding path of teaching and learning.

To all of teachers I've met along the way, thanks for showing me more about how to be an educator with your instructional triumphs and flops than any books or coursework ever could. I'm grateful to my third-grade teacher for instilling a love of literature. To my fifth-grade teacher for bringing creative dramatics to life in class. And to my favorite high school English teacher who really listened, while igniting my passion for poetry. To the handfuls of amazing professors at Chatham College, who collectively taught me what it means to follow your bliss, building my confidence, clarity, and voice. And special thanks to Lynne and Bill for drawing out the very best in me. To my master's level professors at Pitt, thanks for showing me that becoming a teacher happens in the doing, not merely in pondering pedagogy and theory found in textbooks.

A special thank you to Gary, my dissertation advisor at Duquesne University, and now my dear friend. You taught me to only use the very best technologies available, and then only when they could help me to do things not achievable in any other way. To "give away the grade" in order to inspire students to go deeper and produce more meaningful outcomes. To question everything I read, measuring books as "restorative texts" above all else. And to create a safe learning space for students where creativity, innovation, and imagination would flourish.

I'm grateful to Jane, Marie, Megan, and the women of the Red Tent, who've been there for me along the sometimes bumpy road. Your constant friendship through relationship change, job loss, a business launch, new partners, moving, and now the creation of this book, have offered me a deep sense of safety.

Thanks to Doug, Rich, and Elbie, who sat with me as I began to envision the creation of a new kind of school for kids, I offer deep gratitude. Your keen ears, and warm hearts, allowed me to keep on dreaming, even when potential students and parents weren't quite ready to take action.

To my "new-old" Virginia friends: Shannon, Becky, Jessica, Deborrah, Kim, Annie, Airisun, and Shona, your passionate belief in the need for Wisdom Schools truly inspires me. I look forward to many full and happy years working together with you, turning our shared ideas into reality for children all over the planet!

To the Morgan James Publishing team: Special thanks to David Hancock, CEO & Founder for believing in me and my message. To my Author Relations Manager, Gayle West, thanks for making the process seamless and easy. Many more thanks to everyone else, but especially Jim Howard, Bethany Marshall, and Nickcole Watkins.

And a big hug to Chris. I have the deepest of respect for your selfless act in releasing me to craft this book as a catalyst for the next phase of my life. It would have been so much easier for you say nothing at all… versus taking the time to truly see me, to speak your truth, and honor the woman I am becoming!

About the Author

Mara Linaberger's essential belief is that each of us has chosen to be here on the planet at this moment in time for a specific reason. That we're all here on a personal mission of growth and development that we each chose for ourselves prior to our birth.

She believes that figuring out what it is that we love, what we're good at, and why we've chosen to be here now, is the main reason to engage in deep and individualized learning throughout a lifetime. Mara believes that many of today's educational practices actually slow down or stifle those outcomes for many children. So she's become a passionate champion for teachers' utilization of new methods to motivate learning, in order to help students develop to their highest potential.

Mara is a life-long educator, author, musician, and artist, having spent 25 years in service as a public school educator, teacher trainer, and administrator. Earning a Master of Arts in Teaching degree in elementary education, and then an educational doctorate in Instructional Technology, Mara also holds a Superintendent's Letter of Eligibility in the state of Pennsylvania.

Having spent most of her professional career in public school systems, Mara recently sensed it was time to change direction. Launching *Mindful Technology Consultants* in 2013, she now crafts individualized training and support services for small businesses, school districts, and larger educational organizations. Focusing closely on the simplified and intentional use of technology, she helps her clients to deconstruct complex language and ideas in order to achieve harmony, to make rich connections between like-minded entrepreneurs, and to bring back a love for creativity and learning.

Mara currently maintains a small apartment in her hometown that her friends jokingly refer to as "the Pittsburgh hotel room." She travels extensively, tackling unique educational projects and supporting awakened parents and kids in transforming their experiences with education and school. Her latest passion is serving communities ready to design and build a micro-school, transforming thought into reality!

You can reach Mara at: mlinaberger@gmail.com

Thank You!

If you've read this far, THANK YOU. I know everyone doesn't read books from front to back anymore! So if you've stuck in it with me, I have a couple of gifts to offer as a thank you!

In the book I shared several worksheets as part of our exercises. I'd love to send them to you in digital form. And I've also created a companion video series to go with this book. To get both of those freebies, visit my website: http://maralinaberger.com or send me an email.

And last but not least. Would you like to talk about your child's specific situation and get my professional support or input? Send me an email at mlinaberger@gmail.com and we'll book a call to see how I can help!